NATIVE SHRUBS

OF

THE SAN FRANCISCO BAY REGION

BY

ROXANA S. FERRIS

BERKELEY AND LOS ANGELES 1968
UNIVERSITY OF CALIFORNIA PRESS

University of California Press
Berkeley and Los Angeles, California

©1968 by The Regents of the University of California
Library of Congress Catalog Card Number: 68-63190
Printed in the United States of America

CONTENTS

Illustration on Cover:
Leatherwood (*Dirca occidentalis*)

SAN FRANCISCO BAY REGION

INTRODUCTION

The San Francisco Bay Region is rich in shrubs. This area, as defined in earlier California Natural History Guides, comprises the nine Bay counties that touch San Francisco Bay somewhere along its circumference, and Santa Cruz County. (See Map.) When we consider how much of these ten counties is truly urban—major and minor cities with their attendant urban sprawl, and the cultivated land that still remains —it may seem an exaggeration to say that the area is rich in shrubs. The parks (federal, state, town, and county) are many, however, and offer varied plant habitats in their natural state. For habitats associated with surface water there is both salt and fresh. Salt marsh and ocean strand have many more sub-shrubs and woody-based perennials than shrubs, but some do grow there, usually with a depressed growth form. The coastal scrub is rich in shrubs and, though it does not grow at the salt and brackish waterline, it is adjacent to it and benefits by ocean fog and moisture-laden winds. Freshwater lagoons and man-made reservoirs, watercourses and springs give freshwater habitats. Here many kinds of shrubs grow abundantly, usually of the type that is found on north-facing slopes. Some wild gooseberries, Osoberry, Coast Elderberry, azalea, and others are examples of these types. Willows and perhaps ledum, however, are strictly limited to a permanently wet environment.

In dry areas, chaparral is composed almost entirely of shrubs, and much park acreage and some privately owned land can be so classified. The shrub flora is scant in density and in kinds of shrubs in the open oak woodland that still remains, but it is much more dense in the closed-cone pine forest, the redwood forest, and the mixed broad-leaved and Douglas Fir forests.

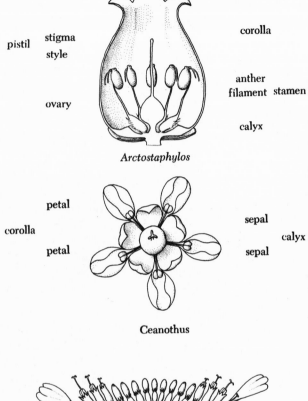

pistil   stigma
         style   corolla

         ovary   anther
                                                  filament   stamen

                                                  calyx

Arctostaphylos

         petal
                                                  sepal
corolla
                                                          calyx
         petal   sepal

Ceanothus

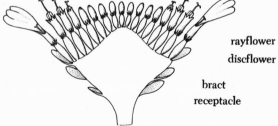

                                                  rayflower
                                                  discflower

                                                  bract
                                                  receptacle

Compositae
Parts of Flowers of Shrubs

ABOUT SHRUBS

The dictionary tells us that a shrub is a "low, usually several stemmed woody plant, or a bush," and a tree is a "woody perennial plant having a single main axis (trunk) usually exceeding 10 feet." Growth patterns in nature are not so precise. The categories shrub, vine, perennnial herb, or tree appear to be self-evident, but the California Buckeye, called "tree" by everyone, does not have a "single main axis," and the live oaks near the ocean squat on strong woody branches and do not attain great height. Conversely, many shrubs may have single stems (trunks), and frequently are more than 10 feet in height (some species of ceanothus, Western Hop Tree, Golden Fleece, and others.)

Nor can a sharp line be drawn between shrub and perennial herb. Many low-growing rock plants (cushion plants) are completely woody. There are dwarf shrubs or sub-shrubs (some species of ceanothus), suffruticose perennials woody only at the base and sending up herbaceous shoots each year. Woody vines, either climbing or trailing, are to be evaluated by the "shrub" definition. With a few exceptions, Howard E. McMinn's *Illustrated Manual of California Shrubs* (University of California Press, 1939) is used as an arbitrary basis in selecting the shrubs of the Bay Region. Among the plants that are included by McMinn and omitted in this guide are: Western Whipplea (*Whipplea modesta*), which has slender trailing stems; and Climbing Bedstraw (*Galium nuttallii*), which climbs a few feet high by even more threadlike stems. The familiar Yerba Buena (*Satureja douglasii*), a trailing plant which usually does not die back to the root, is omitted in both books. Paintbrush (*Cas-*

tilleja) and Coyote Mint (*Monardella*), both exhibiting some woodiness at the base of the plant combined with herbaceous upper parts of annual growth, are excluded here.

LEARNING ABOUT PLANTS AND PLACES

This Guide gives the names of the shrubs of the Bay Region, with some information about each, and line drawings and color prints of many of them. With this as a basis you should seek further for facts about shrubs, and trees and herbs as well, in more comprehensive works written on the California flora. Some of the technical studies, and popular works also, treat the flora of the whole state or segments of it, but others apply only to the Bay Region. They furnish the textbooks for your homework. Of the more technical ones, the most recent on the flora of all of California, *A California Flora* (University of California Press, 1959), was written by Philip A. Munz. Supplement this with McMinn's *Illustrated Manual of California Shrubs* (University of California Press, 1939). (See their glossaries for definitions of technical terms.) Several regional lists have been published in journals or as pamphlets. These three will be helpful as supplements to this Guide: Mary L. Bowerman, *The Flowering Plants and Ferns of Mt. Diablo* (Berkeley: Gillick Press, 1944); John Thomas Howell, *Marin Flora* (University of California Press, 1949); John H. Thomas, *Flora of the Santa Cruz Mountains* (Stanford University Press, 1961).

For field observations on foot, travel light. You will need a bag; your Guide; a large-scale map of the area, and a U. S. Geological Survey topographic map for information on elevations; a combined sketchbook and notebook; a pencil box, and Scotch tape to attach leaves or flowers to your pages of sketches and notes on shrubs; and a hand lens which will give a new outlook on blossoms of creambush, let us say, or the tiny flowers that make up the heads of plants of the sunflower family.

Driving along our county roads instead of walking along the trails of the many state parks and the Point Reyes National Seashore offers a different approach to nature study. County, regional, or recreational maps are readily available from automobile associations, service stations, and offices of federal or state conserved lands. Armed with these maps, make trips from the ocean to the eastern border of the Bay Region counties, always choosing the secondary roads, and plot on the maps the areas where shrubs are seen. Note whether shrubs are common or scarce, associated with trees or not, made up of one kind of shrub or many kinds. It is better to be a passenger than a driver, as you map out shrubby places. The best roads for your purpose are usually curving and narrow and often steep.

The *Introduction to the Natural History of the San Francisco Bay Region* (University of California Press, 1968), gives a list of biotic communities which represent the occurrence of certain plants and animals in certain areas—redwood forest or coastal salt marsh, for example. A more detailed list of plant communities for the whole state is found in Munz' *A California Flora* (University of California Press, 1959), which discusses one of the basic reasons—weather (rainfall, temperature, light)—why plants grow together in one community. Other criteria are used in classifying vegetation, and other names are given to associations of plants. Mary L. Bowerman's *Flowering Plants and Ferns of Mt. Diablo* and Helen K. Sharsmith's *Flora of the Mt. Hamilton Range*[*] include data on what grows characteristically in each plant association or community, and from the complete plant assemblage you can select the shrubs. If you should start at the Santa Clara County border, let us say, driving over the shoulder of Mount Hamilton to an elevation of more

[*]Not in book form but published in *American Midland Naturalist*, vol. 34 (1945): 289-367.

than 4,000 feet, down through urban and rural San Jose to Saratoga, then northward on the Skyline on the crest of the Santa Cruz Mountains, taking the westward road to Pescadero at the ocean, your route would cover all the plant communities in which shrubs are found. Other transects will be equally rewarding. The following list of shrub habitats will serve as a guide: coastal strand, northern coastal scrub, closed-cone pine forest, Douglas Fir forest, Ponderosa Pine forest, redwood forest, mixed evergreen forest, oak woodland, chaparral, and riparian woodland.

The shrub species stray from one community to another to a certain extent. For example, California Burning Bush is typical of redwood forest, but can also be found in closed-cone pine and Douglas Fir forests, but never in chaparral or open oak woodland. In contrast, Poison Oak grows in each of the communities, often in great abundance. Chamise is only in chaparral and very common there, but Mock Heather is limited to the coastal strand. The dark green mounds formed by the many leafless stems of Mexican Tea (*Ephedra californica*), for example, might yet be seen within our borders, as it has been reported from San Joaquin County well north of its normal range. It would represent the only shrubby species of the cone-bearing plants (Coniferophyta) in the Bay Region.

ACKNOWLEDGMENTS
The line drawings of the shrubs in this volume, with the exception of the illustration on page 6, are reprinted with permission of the publishers, Stanford University Press, from *Illustrated Flora of the Pacific States*, Volumes I through IV, by LeRoy Abrams and Roxana S. Ferris; copyright 1923, 1940, 1944, 1951, and 1960 by the Board of Trustees of the Leland Stanford Junior University. The cover illustration and the figure on page 6 were drawn by Kay Brown.

[11]

Many of the colored illustrations were made possible by the loan of transparencies from Jepson Herbarium; the others, except those made by the author, were loaned from the collections of the California Academy of Sciences, and of Dr. R. Hewlett Lee and Dr. John H. Thomas.

DESCRIPTIVE LIST OF SHRUBS
OF THE SAN FRANCISCO BAY REGION

(The families are listed in the same sequence as those in Philip A. Munz's *A California Flora.*)

Fig. 1 Spicebush   Fig. 2 Chaparral Clematis

CALYCANTHUS FAMILY (Calycanthaceae)

Spicebush or **Sweet-shrub** (*Calycanthus occidentalis*), fig. 1, pl. 1a.

This attractive shrub is very much like its eastern relative. It really should not be called "sweet-shrub" in the West; the odor of its maroon flowers and crushed leaves is not sweet but distinctly winy, slightly aromatic. The chrysanthemum-shaped flowers (about 1 to 1½ inches broad) blossom on branchlet tips after the broad entire leaves are fully expanded and continue almost to the time when the leaves turn yellow in autumn. The dry fruit is thimble-shaped. The spreading shrubs, 6 to 10 feet high, are found occasionally in the Bay Region along watercourses in the Coast Ranges north of Marin County.

[13]

BUTTERCUP FAMILY (Ranunculaceae)

Chaparral Clematis or **Virgin's Bower** (*Clematis lasiantha*), fig. 2, pl. 1*b*.

This woody vine is usually found clambering over shrubs in chaparral. The creamy-white axillary flowers, solitary or in clusters of two or more, are fully as attractive as some garden forms. Another species, Western Virgin's Bower (*Clematis ligusticifolia*) (pl. 1*c*), is just as common, but is found along stream banks or moist north-facing slopes. Its flowers, although comparatively small, are conspicuous in their many-flowered clusters. On both species the fruiting heads are made up of many seeds, each with a long plumose tail which makes the head look like an elaborate powder puff.

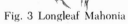

Fig. 3 Longleaf Mahonia   Fig. 4 California Mahonia

BARBERRY FAMILY (Berberidaceae)

Oregon Grape or **Mahonia** (*Mahonia*)

All three species of *Mahonia* growing in the Bay Region have distinctive appearances as well as characteristic habitats. The Long-leaf Mahonia (*M. nervosa*) (fig. 3) grows in forests and is at its best among the redwoods, where it may be 6 feet high instead of the usual 1 or 2 feet. Shiny-leaf or California Mahonia

[14]

(*M. pinnata*) makes occasional clumps on the open slopes of the coastal hills. Jepson's Mahonia (*M. dictyota*), which is also called California Mahonia (fig. 4), displays its blue-green stiff leaflets in mixed chaparral in the Inner Coast Range, but it is not common. All have clusters of yellow flowers and evergreen leaves and, like the rest of the barberries, have yellow wood. All our local ones have blue bloom-covered berries. Those of the Long-leaf Mahonia, densely set on short racemes among the dark shining green clustered leaves, are the most decorative and the tastiest as well; they make a fine jelly. The leaflets of *M. nervosa* are many and lie flat along the stalklike divisions on a fern frond; the other two have fewer leaflets, which are contorted and have prominent spiny margins. The leaves of the coastal species are a shining bright green; those of Jepson's Mahonia are dull-surfaced and usually have a bluish hue. The genus *Mahonia* is sometimes included in *Berberis*, the barberry.

CACAO OR STERCULIA FAMILY (Sterculiaceae)
Flannel-Bush (*Fremontodendron*), pl. 1*d*.

This sturdy shrub grows 4 to 20 feet in height. *Fremontodendron californicum napense*, which grows in the Inner Coast Range north of San Francisco Bay, has slender twigs, leaves ½ to 1 inch long and scarcely lobed, and a bright yellow calyx 1½ inches broad or less. *Fremontodendron* has no true petals. *Fremontodendron californicum crassifolium* grows in mixed chaparral in Santa Clara and Alameda counties. The leaves are thicker, larger, and definitely lobed, and the flowers are 2 inches or more broad. Both forms have evergreen leaves with a very short rough hairiness that is unpleasant to the touch. The woody capsule which opens from the top is especially bristly. It is a great addition to a garden when placed in sunny situations.

Fig. 5 *Malacothamnus arcuatus*   Fig. 6 *Malacothamnus hallii*

MALLOW FAMILY (Malvaceae)

This family is represented in California with fourteen genera. Two shrubby genera occur in the Bay Region. The family includes many garden "familiars" such as hollyhock and hibiscus. In all of them the stamens are united in a tube around the pistil, and the anthers and partly free filaments form a little brush in the center of the flower.

Malacothamnus (*Malacothamnus*)

The three species that occur in the Bay Region are restricted in distribution and never found in extensive stands. All are tough, flexible-stemmed shrubs about 2 to 5 feet high; all have pale pink flowers in tight or open clusters along the flowering stems. *Malacothamnus arcuatus* (fig. 5), is found on the inner slopes of the Outer Coast Range; *M. hallii* (fig. 6), and *M. fremontii cercophorus* grow on Mount Diablo and southward through the Mount Hamilton Range.

Tree-Mallow (*Lavatera*)

Lavatera arborea is a weedy erect shrub, 3 to 6 feet high, with leaves of a velvety texture and clusters of purple flowers in the leaf axils. It is found on ocean bluffs from San Mateo northward. Malva Rosa (*Lavatera assurgentiflora*) (fig. 7), which can grow to a height of 20 feet, has been used in cultivation in the coastal area. A native of the Channel Islands, it has become naturalized to a certain extent, and is sometimes seen in the river area in Contra Costa and Solano counties.

Although *Polygala californica* (pl. 2*a*), of the milkwort family is included with its more shrubby relatives, in McMinn's *Illustrated Manual of California Shrubs,* it is really a herbaceous spreading perennial slightly woody at the base. It is 2 to 12 inches high, with rose-purple flowers and simple dark green leaves.

Fig. 7 Malva Rosa   Fig. 8 Rock-Rose

Spurge Family (Euphorbiaceae)

Castor Bean (*Ricinus communis*)

The well-known Castor Bean occasionally grows spontaneously in waste places and, if not mowed down by frost, becomes a good-sized shrub. The large glossy maple-shaped leaves, reddish stems, and bright red stigmas of the female flowers make it a true ornamental.

Rock-Rose Family (Cistaceae)

Rock-Rose or **Rush-Rose** (*Helianthemum scoparium*), fig. 8.

This small shrub, 6 to 18 inches high, is found on sunny slopes. During most of the year it is a broom-like mass of erect twigs from its woody crown. The small linear ½ inch leaves are soon deciduous. The bright yellow flowers in the axils of the upper leaves, though small, are conspicuous in their abundance.

Elsewhere in California members of the genus *Tamarix* in the tamarisk family have become naturalized. *Tamarix tetrandra,* a woody shrub covered in spring, before the scalelike leaves come out, with myriads of tiny pink flowers, may be expected to occur near old habitations in the Inner Coast Range. It has been reported from Corral Hollow Road on the eastern edge of Alameda County.

Fig. 9 Alkali-heath   Fig. 10 Tree Poppy

Frankenia Family (Frankeniaceae)

Alkali-heath or Frankenia (*Frankenia grandifolia*) (fig. 9) is a low sprawling sub-shrub very common in salt marshes and found in other situations where there is alkalinity in the soil. Alkali-heath appears to be more frequently herblike than shrublike, as it spreads by its woody stems as a ground cover in the salt marshes where it is associated with pickleweed (*Salicornia virginica*). The small gray leaves are opposite—whorled on older stems—and the small pink flowers grow in the leaf axils.

POPPY FAMILY (Papaveraceae)

Tree Poppy (*Dendromecon rigidum*), fig. 10, pl. 2*b*.

On mixed chaparral slopes the occasional plants in full bloom are a pleasing sight. The clear yellow flowers are 1½ to 2 inches broad. The alternate, elliptic, evergreen leaves are firm and blue-green, and grow sparsely along the stiff branches of the shrub, which is 3 to 8 feet high. Tree poppies vary considerably in their occurrence throughout the state.

Sea-fig (*Mesembryanthemum chilense*)

A widely creeping, magenta-flowered, angular-leaved vine is this coarse succulent of the sand dunes. It is not considered among the lesser sub-shrubs and creepers in *Illustrated Manual of California Shrubs,* but is more conspicuous than many that are included. The closely related yellow-flowered *M. edule* planted along roadcuts and banks to control erosion is a familiar sight.

BUCKWHEAT FAMILY (Polygonaceae)

California Buckwheat or **Flat-top** (*Eriogonum fasciculatum*), fig. 11.

Many herbaceous species of *Eriogonum* occur in the Bay Region counties, but the only truly shrubby species here is *E. fasciculatum foliolosum*. The small narrow leaves are clustered at each joint on the spreading woody branches. The margins of each dark green leaf are strongly inrolled and partially conceal the white undersurface. The leafy stems and the flower stems branch widely; on the tips of each branchlet close clusters of tiny white flowers are borne. Santa Cruz and Santa Clara counties are the northern limits of this particular form of *E. fasciculatum*. This and other subspecies are widespread in California in coastal mountain ranges or interior deserts. It has been used in highway roadcuts in arid places.

Fig. 11 California Buckwheat   Fig. 12 Brewer's Salt Bush

Fig. 13 Bush Pickleweed   Fig. 14 Alkali-blite fruiticosa

GOOSEFOOT OR SALTBUSH FAMILY (Chenopodiaceae) A large family well represented in the West by many native species of saltbush (*Atriplex*), pigweed (*Chenopodium*), both native and naturalized species, pickleweed (*Salicornia*), and even beet or beet root (*Beta*) which has escaped from truck gardens and

[20]

established itself in disturbed areas. Most of the species in the family demand or tolerate alkaline conditions for best growth.

Brewer's or **Coast Salt Bush** (*Atriplex lentiformis breweri*), fig. 12.

This grows from Solano County southward through the coastal ranges to southern California. The bushes are 3 to 10 feet high and equally broad, and are covered abundantly with gray simple, short-stalked leaves, 1 to 2 inches long. The male and female flowers are separated. The male flowers form a mass of many stamens. Female flowers (no petals or sepals) in branched hanging clusters are completely enclosed by a pair of flat rounded bracts. This subspecies has been used in gardens, as the plants are attractive and easy to grow.

Bush Pickleweed or **Iodine Bush** (*Allenrolfea occidentalis*), fig. 13.

Allenrolfea occidentalis, like the common pickleweed of the salt marshes, has no evident leaves to show on the completely fleshy alternate branches. The woody stems making up this sprawling shrub are 1½ to 4 feet high. In the Bay counties it is found in alkaline seeps in inner Contra Costa and Santa Clara counties. Sea-blite or seep weed, species of the genus *Suaeda*, have fleshy leaves instead of fleshy stems, and grow in similar situations. California Sea-blite (*S. californica*) is a denizen of alkaline places along the seacoast, while the shrubby-based perennial, Alkali-blite (*S. fruticosa*) (fig. 14) grows in alkaline places on the eastern face of the Inner Coast Range.

HEATHER FAMILY (Ericaceae)

Some genera and several species in this family are native to the Bay Region. All the genera have undivided leaves. All have evergreen leaves except *Rhododendron occidentale*, the Western Azalea, and *Vaccin-*

Fig. 15 Red Huckleberry   Fig. 16 Salal Berry

Fig. 17 Labrador Tea   Fig. 18 *Vaccinium ovatum*

ium parvifolium, Red Huckleberry (fig. 15, pl. 2c).
If the material you wish to know about is in fruit,
only three of the genera will have berries. Huckle-
berries (*Vaccinium*) and Salal Berry (*Gaultheria shallon*) (fig. 16) will have juicy or fleshy berries, and
manzanitas (*Arctostaphylos*) will have dry berries
with a granular pulp. Two genera have dry capsules:
Ledum glandulosum columbianum (Labrador Tea)

[22]

(fig. 17, pl. 2d), with capsules splitting open from the bottom; and *Rhododendron*, with larger capsules that split open from the top. If your material is in flower only, it is still quite easy to name the genus. If the clustered flowers are rather small with flatly spreading petals, it is ledum. If the flowers are large with petals broadly bell-shaped and rose-purple, or funnel-shaped and white (or pink tinged) blotched with yellow, it is the genus *Rhododendron*. If the flowers have no evident petals, are small and fused into an urn-like shape, you have either *Arctostaphylos*, *Vaccinium ovatum* (fig. 18), or *Gaultheria*. The flowers are in rather compact clusters in manzanita; larger and in a loose raceme in Salal Berry, and solitary or in clusters in the leaf axils in the huckleberry. With the exception of some of the many species of manzanita, the genera of the heather family that grow in the Bay Region occur in counties of the immediate coast.

Manzanita (*Arctostaphylos*)

Arctostaphylos, like *Ceanothus*, is one of the larger genera in number of species in the state, and many of the species grow in the Bay Region counties. The growth form is variable: some kinds are creepers, some form mounds and have trailing branches that root readily, some are erect branching shrubs 10 to 20 feet high. Some of the erect shrubs are killed by fire, but others of the shrubby species sprout again after fire from a woody basal platform or burl. One finds a conspicuous lack of unanimity in the scientific names applied to manzanitas in the books on western plants. One botanist's species may be only a subspecies or even a synonym in another botanist's opinion. It would appear that not all the species—often hybrids that occur in nature—are yet stabilized and thus have not had time to spread into adjacent localities. Quite a few that are recognizably distinct are very

Fig. 19 *Arctostaphylos silvicola* Fig. 20 Bigberried Manzanita

limited in distribution, such as *A. silvicola* (fig. 19),
which grows only in a small area in Santa Cruz
County, and *A. crustacea rosei*, which is found only
in the coastal scrub in San Francisco County. Other
species, like the Big-berried Manzanita (*A. glauca*)
(fig. 20), seem "old" and well established. Big-berried
Manzanita has an extensive range from Mount Diablo
southward to Baja California. For your convenience
all the species known to grow in the ten Bay Region
counties are listed here by growth form. For convenience, also, the scientific names in the lists are
taken from one book only: *A California Flora* by Philip A. Munz. Should this flora be unavailable, you
may find the name you seek in other books.* It may
not be the same category you find in the Munz flora,
which was published in 1959. Instead of being a species it may be a synonym, but you can at least match

*L. R. Abrams, *Illustrated Flora of the Pacific States*, vol. 3
(Stanford University Press, 1951); W. L. Jepson, *A Manual
of the Flowering Plants of California* (University of California
Press, repr. 1966); Howard E. McMinn, *An Illustrated Manual
of California Shrubs* (University of California Press, 1939);
and other manuals of a more limited range.

the name with the information given about the plant
in the book that you have in hand.

Fig. 21 *Arctostaphylos
densiflora*

Fig. 22 *Arctostaphylos
stanfordiana*

*Plants creeping or forming low mounds a foot or more high;
branches usually rooting on contact with soil:*

Arctostaphylos densiflora...Local; west of Santa Rosa, Sonoma
(fig. 21)   Co.
A. hookeri franciscana.....Local; San Francisco peninsula
A. nummularia...........Closed-cone pine forest (damp
                          places); Sonoma Co. north to Men-
                          docino Co.
A. nummularia sensitiva   Chaparral, mixed evergreen for-
(2 to 6 feet high)   est; Marin Co. south to Santa
                               Cruz Co.
A. pungens montana.......Chaparral, serpentine slopes; Ma-
                          rin Co.
A. uva-ursi coactilis.......Coastal strand; San Bruno Mt.,
                           San Mateo Co., Point Reyes, Ma-
                           rin Co., north

*Plants not moundlike, branches more or less erect, not usually
rooting on contact with soil:*

Plants having woody basal platform or burls; sprouting after
fire.

A. crustacea..............Chaparral; Contra Costa Co. south
                          to Santa Barbara Co.

A. *crustacea rosei*......... Local, coastal scrub; San Francisco Co.

A. *glandulosa*............ Chaparral, mixed evergreen forest; coastal ranges throughout state

A. *glandulosa campbelliae*.. Local, chaparral; Mt. Hamilton, Santa Clara Co.

A. *glandulosa cushingiana*   Dry mixed evergreen forest, chaparral; Marin Co., Napa Co., Sonoma Co.

A. *tomentosa tomenotosi-*
formis .... Local, closed-cone pine forest; Año Nuevo Point, San Mateo Co. to San Luis Obispo Co.

Plants not having a basal burl; killed outright by fire

A. *andersonii*............ Mixed evergreen forest, chaparral; San Francisco Co. south to Santa Lucia Mts.

A. *andersonii imbricata*.... Local, coastal scrub; San Bruno Mt., San Mateo Co.

A. *andersonii pallida*...... Local, chaparral; Mt. Diablo region, Alameda Co. and Contra Costa Co.

A. *auriculata*............ Local, chaparral; Mt. Diablo region, Alameda Co. and Contra Costa Co.

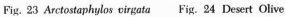

Fig. 23 *Arctostaphylos virgata*   Fig. 24 Desert Olive

A. *canescens*	Yellow-pine forest; Santa Cruz Co. and Santa Clara Co. north to Oregon border
A. *canescens candidissima* . .	Yellow-pine forest; Napa Co. north to Trinity Co. and Tehama Co.
A. *canescens sonomensis* . . .	Local; near Santa Rosa, Sonoma Co.
A. *columbiana*	Coastal scrub; Sonoma Co. north to British Columbia
A. *glauca* (often treelike . . . to 18 feet)	Chaparral; Inner Coast Range from Mt. Diablo south to Baja California
A. *glutinosa*	Local, chaparral; west of Bonnie Doon Ridge, Santa Cruz Co.
A. *manzanita*	Chaparral, oak woodland, etc.; Contra Costa Co. north to Oregon border
A. *manzanita laevigata*	Local; slopes of Mt. Diablo and Mt. St. Helena
A. *silvicola*	Local, yellow-pine forest; Mt. Hermon, Santa Cruz Co.
A. *stanfordiana* (fig. 22 . . . pl. 3*a*)	Chaparral; Napa Co. and Sonoma Co. north to Mendocino Co. and Lake Co.
A. *stanfordiana bakeri*	Local, serpentine ridges; Sonoma Co.
A. *virgata* (fig. 23)	Local, closed-cone pine forest, mixed evergreen forest; Marin Co.
A. *viscida*	Chaparral, yellow-pine forest; Napa Co. north to Oregon

OLIVE FAMILY (Oleaceae)

Desert Olive (*Forestiera*), fig. 24.

Forestiera neomexicana is a deciduous shrub of wide distribution, ranging as far east as Texas. Within our limits it is found sparingly in hot interior valleys of the Coast Ranges in dry arroyos on the eastern side of the Hamilton Range.

The shrubs, as tall as 9 feet, are spiny-branched. The narrow simple leaves are 1 to 1½ inches long. The staminate and the pistillate flowers have no petals and are in small bunches. The elliptic fruit is blue-black and somewhat fleshy.

[27]

WATERLEAF OR PHACELIA FAMILY (Hydrophyllaceae)

California Yerba Santa (*Eriodictyon californicum*), fig. 25, pl. 3*b*.

Seven species of *Eriodictyon* are found in various places throughout the state. But only one of these, California Yerba Santa, is found in the Bay Region, although it is not limited to that area, as it grows naturally from the Oregon border south to Kern and San Luis Obispo counties in mixed chaparral and mixed evergreen forest in dry situations. A weedy growth of stems 2 to 8 feet high from an underground rootstock, with sticky branchlets and thick willow-shaped leaves, characterizes the yerba santa that grows locally. The leaves, toothed on the margin, are sticky above and dull white below. The branching clusters of pale purple trumpet-shaped flowers come in late spring or early summer. A brew of the aromatic shrub was used by early pioneers and Indians as a cure for respiratory diseases.

NIGHTSHADE FAMILY (Solanaceae)

Tree Tobacco (*Nicotiana glauca*), fig. 26.

This South American tobacco is the only shrubby species in California. It is widely naturalized on streambanks and waste places in the interior valleys of the Coast Ranges and in similar situations throughout the state. The loosely branching, slender-stemmed shrub can grow to more than 15 feet; the entire green leaves, faintly bluish in tone, are long-stalked; the yellow tubular flowers, 1½ inches long, are in loose clusters. The fruit is a dry capsule.

Nightshade (*Solanum*)

The genus *Solanum* is well represented in California, partly by naturalized weeds, partly by native species. In its worldwide distribution it is one of the larger genera, having about 1,000 species.

Blue Witch or **Nightshade** (*Solanum umbelliferum*), fig. 27, pl. 3*c*.

This is a leafy rounded shrub up to 3 feet and more in height, often merely woody at the base. The short-stalked gray-green leaves are from 1 to nearly 2 inches long. A variety with leaves strongly whitened with hairs is found from the Inner Coast Range southward.

Fig. 25 California Yerba Santa

Fig. 26 Tree Tobacco

Fig. 27 Blue Witch

Fig. 28 White-margined nightshade

Two other shrubby species have escaped from cultivation in the Bay Region. Both have much larger leaves than Blue Witch. Poporo (*S. aviculare*) has no hairs on the willow-shaped leaves, which may be entire or have three or four widely spreading narrow lobes. White-margined Nightshade (*S. marginatum*) (fig. 28) has wavy-margined leaves spiny along the veins and a velvety undersurface.

FIGWORT FAMILY (Scrophulariaceae)

The shrubby veronica of the genus *Hebe* has been reported to have escaped from gardens.

Sticky Monkeyflower (*Mimulus aurantiacus*), fig. 29, pl. 3*d*.

This shrub is 1½ to 3 feet high, branching from the woody base. The erect branches are clothed with narrow opposite leaves which are sticky on the upper surface. The orange-yellow funnel-shaped flowers, 1½ inch long, are in the axils of the leaves. The blooming period lasts from spring through summer; the later flowers come on new growth from the woody base. It is one of the most common small shrubs found in open places in woodland and chaparral in the Bay Region.

Beardstongue (*Penstemon*)

Some of the prettiest western perennials are beardstongues. A few of the species are used in cultivation for borders and rock gardens. The colors are varied, ranging through red and pink to blue and white. Among the few western species that are classed as shrubs, two are found in the Bay Region. *Penstemon corymbosus*, variously called Thyme-leaf Penstemon and Redwood Penstemon (fig. 30), is found on rocky hilltops and cliffs. The leafy spreading branches are about 1½ feet long and inclined to mat. The showy brick-red tubular flowers are 1½ inches long and clustered terminally on the branches. *Penstemon bre-*

viflorus (Gaping Penstemon, or Bush Beardstongue), (fig. 31, pl. 4*a*), grows 1 to 3 feet high. The erect stems are slender and often herbaceous; the leaves are small and sparse along the stems and branches. The short ½ inch flowers are in loose branching panicles; they are white with pink or purple markings and, like the preceding, two-lipped. It grows on rocky shrubby slopes throughout the state, but is not very common.

Fig. 29 Sticky Monkeyflower

Fig. 30 Redwood Penstemon

Fig. 31 Gaping Penstemon

Fig. 32 Black Sage

MINT FAMILY (Labiatae)

The most obvious characteristic of this family is the aroma given out by the foliage. Many of the culinary herbs belong in this family, such as basil, mint, lemon balm, and rosemary. The leaves are always opposite and the stems usually four-angled. The yellow-flowered Jerusalem Sage (*Phlomis fruticosa*) and Lions-ear (*Leonotus leonurus*), which has orange-yellow spikes of flowers, are sub-shrubs that have escaped from gardens and maintain themselves to a degree without cultivation.

Sage (*Salvia*)

The large genus *Salvia* grows in both hemispheres, mostly in temperate regions. It is represented in California by about twenty species of annuals, perennials, or shrubs. The shrubby species are well represented in southern California, some of them very attractive and suitable for cultivation.

The only shrubby sage of the Bay Region is the widespread Black Sage (*S. mellifera*) (fig. 32). This shrub, which is found on dry slopes in mixed chaparral, is 2 to 3 feet high. The spikes on the inflorescense rise well above the leaf-covered branches. The small pale lavender of whitish flowers are in tight, widely spaced whorls. It is an excellent bee plant. Sonoma or Creeping Sage (*S. sonomensis*), which is classed as a shrub by some, has woody matted leaf-covered stems. The leafless erect spikes bear whorls of violet-blue flowers. It is found in scattered localities throughout the state on dry ridges and slopes.

Pitcher Sage (*Lepechinia calycina*), fig. 33, pl. 4*b*.

In contrast to the salvias, the aromatic foliage of Pitcher Sage is rather repellent. The shrubs are about 3 feet high. The leafy-bracted white flowers (with purple markings) are 1 inch long, set in a loose puffy calyx. It is found in our area in mixed woodland or

a) Spicebush

  Calycanthus occidentalis

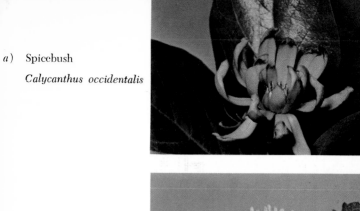

b) Chaparral Clematis

  Clematis lasiantha

c) Western Virgin's Bower

  Clematis ligusticifolia

d) Flannel-Bush

  Fremontodendron californicum

PLATE 1

a) *Polygala californica*

b) Tree Poppy

Dendromecon rigidum

c) Red Huckleberry

Vaccinium parvifolium

d) Labrador Tea

Ledum glandulosum

PLATE 2

a) *Arctostaphylos*
      stanfordiana

b) California Yerba Santa
      Eriodictyon californicum

c) Blue Nightshade
      Solanum umbelliferum

d) Sticky Monkeyflower
      Mimulus aurantiacus

PLATE 3

a) Gaping Penstemon
Penstemon breviflorus

b) Pitcher Sage
Lepichinia calycina

c) Chaparral
Flowering Currant
Ribes malvaceum

d) California Rose
Rosa Californica

PLATE 4

a) Himalaya Berry
  Rubus procerus

b) Chaparral Pea
  Pickeringia montana

c) Silver Lupine
  Lupinus albifrons

d) California Dutchman's
  Pipe
  Aristolochia californica

PLATE 5

a) Blue Blossom
Ceanothus thyrsiflorus

b) Chaparral Whitethorn
Ceanothus leucodermis

c) Buckbrush
Ceanothus cuneatus

d) Western Hop Tree
Ptelea crenulata

PLATE 6

a) Poison Oak
   Rhus diversiloba

b) Western Dogwood
   Cornus occidentalis

c) Coast Elderberry
   Sambucus pubens

d) Blue Elderberry
   Sambucus mexicana

PLATE 7

a) Lizard Tail

    Eriophyllum staechadifolium

b) Mock Heather

    Haplopappus ericoides

c) Narrowleaf Goldenbush

    Haplopappus linearifolius

d) Chaparral Broom

    Baccharis pilularis

PLATE 8

mixed chaparral, from the Lake County border to
Ventura County.

Fig. 33 Pitcher Sage

Fig. 34 Golden Currant

Fig. 35 Pink Flowering
Currant

Fig. 36 Fuchsia-flowered
Gooseberry

SAXIFRAGE FAMILY (Saxifragaceae)

Gooseberry, Currant (*Ribes*)

Gooseberries and currants are distinct in appearance.
According to some botanists, the gooseberries should
be classified separately under the genus *Grossularia*.
All our species of the "gooseberry" section have strong
spines at the nodes of stems and branches. This char-
acter is lacking in local species of the "currant" section. A variety of the Golden Currant (*Ribes aureum
gracillimum*) (fig. 34) is occasionally seen in the

[33]

SPECIES OF RIBES (GOOSEBERRY)

Species	Description	Habitat	Distribution
Ribes amarum, Bitter Gooseberry	sepals red-purple, berries sticky, bristly	foothill, woodland	reported from Hamilton Range
R. californicum, Hillside Gooseberry	sepals greenish or purple-tinged, berries bristly		Coast Ranges, Mendocino Co. south to Monterey
Ribes divaricatum, Straggly Gooseberry (fig. 37)	sepals mostly greenish, berries smooth	riparian, i.e., streambanks	Coast Ranges, Santa Barbara Co. north
R. menziesii leptosmum, Bay Gooseberry	sepals purplish red, berries bristly	mixed evergreen forest, redwood forest	Sonoma Co., Alameda Co., south Bay Region only
R. menziesii menziesii, Coast Gooseberry (fig. 38)	sepals purplish red, berries bristly	redwood forest, coastal canyons	San Luis Obispo Co. north
R. menziesii senile, Santa Cruz Gooseberry	sepals purplish red, berries soft-hairy, bristles sparse	mixed evergreen forest	more common inland than *R. menziesii menziesii*; local in Santa Cruz Mts.
R. quercetorum (see text), Oak Gooseberry	sepals pale yellow, berries smooth	foothill, woodland	Inner Coast Range, Alameda Co. south
R. roezlii cruentum, Sierra Gooseberry	sepals purplish red, berries spiny	mixed evergreen forest, northern oak woodland	Napa Co. and Sonoma Co.
R. speciosum (see text)			
R. victoris, Victor Gooseberry	sepals purplish, berries red-sticky, bristly	wooded canyons, redwood forest	Bay Region only Marin, Sonoma, Solano, Napa counties.

Fig. 37 Straggly Gooseberry   Fig. 38 Coast Gooseberry

canyons of the Inner Coast Range from Alameda County south. Its nearly glabrous leaf blades have 3 to 5 shallow lobes; the yellow flowers are in small racemes; the smooth berries are reddish orange or occasionally black. The other native currants here have pink-flowered racemes and sticky blue-black fruit. The veiny thickish leaves are more or less hairy and somewhat aromatic with glands. Chaparral Flowering Currant (*R. malvaceum*) (pl. 4c), occurs commonly in dry shrubby places; Pink Flowering Currant (*R. sanguineum glutinosum*) (fig. 35), is more often encountered in redwood and closed-cone pine forests.

The rarest of the species of gooseberries within our limits is by far the most beautiful and has been used as a garden shrub. Fuchsia-flowered Gooseberry (*R. speciosum*) (fig. 36), has been collected a few times only in canyons of ranges flanking the southern end of the Santa Clara Valley, which is its northern limit. The sepals (about ½ inch long) are not reflexed as they are in local species, and both petals and sepals are divided in 4's instead of 5's. The over-all length of the bright red flowers from the bristly ovary to the tips of the anthers is about 2 inches. The flowers, ap-

[35]

pearing singly or in 2's or 3's, are very conspicuous against the glossy dark green, essentially evergreen leaves. The leaves are deciduous on all the others. The flowers of the remaining local species are smaller than those of *R. speciosum*, but they also droop on short stalks from the bases of nodal spines. The reflexed sepals may be purplish or greenish, and the erect petals are whitish with the exception of the Oak Gooseberry (*R. quercetorum*), in which the floral parts are greenish yellow to pale yellow. This species grows more often in open woodland, whereas the other native ones are seen more frequently on north-facing slopes in denser growth. All these gooseberries have arching leafy branches.

Fig. 39 Mountain Mahogany

Fig. 40 Chamise

ROSE FAMILY (Rosaceae)

Shrubs belonging to the rose family are well represented in the Bay Region. This large family includes numerous and varied genera. The different types of fruit and leaves offer one of the obvious ways of telling apart the twelve genera that occur locally.

Mature fruit dry, about ¼ inch long.

[36]

Fruit with 2½ to 3 inch twisted, plumose tail. . . . .
. . . . Mountain Mahogany
Fruit without a long appendage.
    Leaves evergreen, growing in close clusters, about ¼
    inch long, needle-like. . . . . Chamise
    Leaves deciduous, not clustered, 1 to 2 inches wide,
    margins lobed and toothed. . . . . Ninebark, Creambush
Mature fruit fleshy or juicy, the pulp in some but thinly cov-
ering the seeds.
    Leaves compound (merely lobed in Thimbleberry).
    Fruit a red "hip" (urn-shaped, fleshy receptacle) con-
    taining bony seeds. . . . . Rose
    Fruit an aggregate berry (juicy, seeded druplets
    attached to central stalk). . . . . Blackberry, Raspberry,
    Thimbleberry, Salmonberry
    Leaves simple.
    Fruit a drupe (single seed or "stone") more or less
    covered with pulp; dried flower parts if present at
    stem end of fruit. . . . Wild Cherry, Wild Plum, Osoberry
    Fruit a pome (apple-like fleshy fruit containing sev-
    eral seeds); dried flower parts evident on blossom
    (terminal) end of fruit. . . . . Christmas Berry, Service
    Berry, Oregon Crab Apple,
    Hawthorn

Mountain Mahogany (*Cercocarpus betuloides*), fig. 39.

An open shrub, often with a treelike growth form,
found in mixed shrubby growth of hillslopes in both
the Inner and the Outer Coast Range. The small con-
spicuously veined leaves when first crushed give off
a smell of wintergreen.

Chamise (*Adenostoma fasciculatum*), fig. 40.

Chamise is one of the commonest shrubs on chaparral-
covered hillsides, and often this heather-like plant
grows in pure stands. It is a much stiffer-stemmed
shrub than heather and can grow into 3 to 6 foot
thickets that are almost impenetrable. The small white
stalkless flowers are in compact clusters at the ends of
the branches.

Creambush (*Holodiscus discolor*), fig. 41.

Both Creambush and Western Ninebark (*Physocarpus*

Fig. 41 Creambush

Fig. 42 Western Ninebark

Fig. 43 Pine Rose

Fig. 44 Salmonberry

capitatus) (fig. 42), prefer north-facing slopes and moist canyons for a habitat, and both are found in the coast ranges in north and south as well as central parts of California. They have similar alternate deciduous leaves. Both are shreddy-barked erect-stemmed shrubs, which may grow to a height of 12 feet or more. Creambush, or Ocean Spray as it is often called, with its much-branched terminal panicles of cream-colored blossoms, is the more beautiful of the two shrubs as well as the more common. Ninebark has a smaller, more or less flattened inflorescence of white flowers.

Rose (*Rosa*)

The genus *Rosa* is easy to recognize, but the species,

like those of manzanita, are hard to identify. Fortunately, three of the species that occur locally are easily distinguished. All have flowers with rose-pink petals.

Sweetbriar or Eglantine (*Rosa eglantina*)

This is a European species naturalized in many localities of the United States. It has spread from the northern coast along the rolling pasture land near the sea and is by way of becoming a pest. The curved hooked spines on the erect-stemmed clumps are stout and flattened. The scarlet or orange-rose hips are about ¾ of an inch long, not including the attached sepals.

Wood Rose or Redwood Rose (*Rosa gymnocarpa*)

This slender-stemmed straggly shrub is a denizen of forests. In the north it is found in the moister forest of the Outer Coast Range. The leaflets are small; the stems have abundant slender prickles, and the solitary flowers are small and delicately fragrant. It is easy to recognize in fruit because of the small fleshy rose hips, which, unlike the other local species, drop the sepals early.

Sonoma Ground Rose (*Rosa spithamea sonomensis*)

This low-growing rose is found in drier places, even in chaparral, from Sonoma County southward to San Luis Obispo County. Both the sepals and the unripe hips have glandular spreading hairs.

California Rose (*Rosa californica*), pl. 4d.

This, by far our commonest species, often forms thickets along fences or near streams and other moist places. The flowers, seldom solitary, grow in corymbs (a flattened raceme with the lowest flower stems longer and also bearing the first blooms). This common California species is quite variable, and segregate species have been recognized by some botanists. The typical form was first collected long ago in San Francisco. The Pine Rose (*R. pinetorum*) (fig. 43), is occasionally collected on higher slopes in the forest. It is much more common in the Sierra Nevada. It resembles the Redwood Rose, but the sepals of the rose hips are not deciduous.

Blackberry, Raspberry, Thimbleberry, Salmonberry (*Rubus*)

The berries of all the local species of *Rubus* are edible but, with some exceptions, hardly worth the trouble to eat as they are usually dry and seedy. The more luxurious plants of the coastal fog belt tend to be juicier. The California Blackberry is good, but fruits only sparsely. The tasty wild blackberry pies are made from the Himalaya Berry or less often from the Cutleaf Blackberry, which also has escaped from cultivation. The Himalaya Berry (*R. procerus*) (pl. 5a),

Fig. 45 Cutleaf Blackberry   Fig. 46 Hollyleaf Cherry

Fig. 47 Sierra Plum   Fig. 48 Osoberry

[40]

forms mounds of brambles along roadsides and near farms. Salmonberry plants (fig. 44) are confined to coastal draws and canyons from Santa Cruz County northward.

Thimbleberry is common in several habitats: coastal scrub, redwood forest, and riparian situations, and is conspicuous with its large white flowers and broad soft-textured leaves.

California Blackberry occurs in an even greater variety of habitats. Either as a trailing vine or as a low mound it can be seen in closed-cone pine forest, redwood forest, mixed evergreen, yellow-pine forest, coastal scrub, and even open oak woodland.

Western Raspberry sends up canes like the cultivated raspberry, and bears fruit much like the cultivated forms. The young canes are white-stemmed and the backs of the leaflets are white-hairy. It can be found in the mixed evergreen forests on the inner face of the Outer Coast Range and suitable places in the Inner Coast Range.

Petals rose-pink, more or less erect and spreading for the upper third.........Salmonberry (*Rubus spectabilis franciscanus*)
Petals white, spreading horizontally in one plane.

    Leaves maple like, lobes not deeply cut to central leaf
      vein; petals broad, overlapping......................
                          Thimbleberry (*R. parviflorus*)
    Leaves divided into 3 to 5 leaflets (rarely merely lobes
    in *vitifolius*); petals not broad, not overlapping..........
                    California Blackberry (*R. vitifolius* [inc.
      R. ursinus]) Himalaya Berry (*R. procerus*), pl. 5*a*
                    Western Raspberry (*R. leucodermis*),
                    Cutleaf Blackberry (*R. laciniatus*),
                                fig. 45

Stone-Fruits (*Prunus*)

The cherries, peaches, apricots, and plums are known as stone fruits. Four native species of *Prunus* are found locally, and plants of either garden or orchard species may occur naturally as stray plants, probably spread by birds as are *Cotoneaster* and *Pyracantha*.

[41]

The species listed here, with the exception of the Hollyleaf Cherry, are of wide distribution in the West, but are not found in great abundance.

Hollyleaf Cherry (*Prunus ilicifolia*) (fig. 46), is the only one with evergreen leaves. The dark purple, almost black, fruit has a large stone and very little pulp. The three deciduous species, Sierra Plum *P. subcordata*), (fig. 47), Bitter Cherry (*P. emarginata*), and Western Chokecherry (*P. virginiana demissa*), are not often seen. The petals of all local species are white. The inflorescence of Bitter Cherry is a flattened raceme with the lowest branches lengthening and blossoming first (corymb). Western Chokecherry has a densely flowered raceme 2 to 4 inches long. Both are found on wooded slopes and streambanks. Sierra Plum has broad leaves and large fruit (about ¾ of an inch). Variants of the species in northern California make excellent jam and jelly.

Osoberry (*Osomaronia cerasiformis*), fig. 48.

Osoberry can easily be mistaken for wild plum. It is technically separate because of the dioecious flowers (the different sexes [staminate and pistillate] borne on separate plants). Also, the pistils of the pistillate flowers are five instead of one, as in the genus *Prunus*. The willow-shaped leaves are deciduous, and the thin flesh on the fruits of the hanging raceme is very bitter.

Oregon Crab Apple (*Malus fusca*) is considered by McMinn (*Illustrated Manual of California Shrubs*) to be a large shrub, but it is often classified as a tree. It grows along the coast as far south as Sonoma County, but not abundantly.

Service Berry (*Amelanchier pallida*), fig. 49.

These deciduous shrubs are about 3 feet high (sometimes reaching 15 feet) with stiffly spreading branches. The five spreading petals are white. The small fruits, reddish at first and ripening purple, are called "berries," but are constructed like tiny apples (pomes). In some books this species is treated as a

Fig. 49 Service Berry   Fig. 50 Hawthorn

Fig. 51 California Christmas   Fig. 52 Western Redbud
Berry

variety of or merely a synonym of *A. alnifolia*, a species of wide distribution in the West. Sometimes it is considered to be *A. florida*. Evaluation of the species of this genus is difficult. The shrubs are often seen on coastal cliffs in the northern counties or around freshwater ponds behind the dunes.

Hawthorn or **Thorn-apple** (*Crataegus douglasii*), fig. 50.

In the West the few species of hawthorn that are natives are confined mostly to the northern part. The one that is native to California occurs sparingly as far south as Marin County. This hawthorn is a deciduous shrub or even small tree with stems that bear stout brown spines ½ to ¾ of an inch long and leaves with toothed margins. The flowers are white; the purple or black fruit is ½ of an inch or less long.

California Christmas Berry, Toyon (*Heteromeles arbutifolia*), fig. 51.

Locally this is the best known of the rosaceous shrubs either with pomes or stone fruit, for it grows commonly in chaparral as well as on open brushy slopes. Long before the advent of extensive planting of pyracanthas and cotoneasters for floral trimming at Christmas time, Toyon berries were gathered commercially and sold. The short-toothed evergreen leaves and dense flattened clusters (corymbs) of small bright red berry-like pomes are very attractive to people and even more so to wild birds.

PEA FAMILY (Leguminosae)

This is an extremely large family. Some of the genera such as the peas and beans are of economic importance. The genera belonging to two of the three subfamilies are few in California. The largest number of native ones are in the bean subfamily (Papilionoideae), which contains large well-known groups like the clovers, lupines, and locoweeds (*Astragalus*). Including all three subfamilies, not many kinds of shrubs are found growing naturally in the Bay Region, although herbaceous species are well represented. The acacias and albizia (*Albizia distachya*) belong to the mimosa subfamily (*Mimosoideae*) and their local occurrence in the wild is negligible. All these species are in gardens or along highways, and all set viable seed. A few uncultivated plants are occasionally collected.

Western Redbud (*Cercis occidentalis*), fig. 52.

The only representative of the senna subfamily in the Bay Region is a tall shrub or small tree. In spring the bare branches and twigs are closely covered with small, cerise sweetpea-shaped flowers. The leaves that follow are not the characteristic compound leaves of the pea family, but are simple, entire, and almost

Fig. 53 Silver Lupine   Fig. 54 Yellow Bush Lupine

round. The pods are flat and brown. One is fortunate to see it in canyons of Napa and Solano counties, for it is much more common in the foothills of the Sierra Nevada.

Chaparral Pea (*Pickeringia montana*), pl. 5*b*.

Chaparral Pea (sometimes called Stingaree Bush) is a shrub that makes the chaparral even more impenetrable. Although common, it does not grow in great stands. The stiff interlacing branches spread widely, each ending in a strong spiny tip. The bright pink flowers are almost half the size of sweetpeas. It does not seed readily.

Lupine (*Lupinus*)

There are about 100 different kinds of lupines native to California, a few of which are classed as shrubs. In these the palmate compound leaves are deciduous and the wood is quite soft. The shrubs have a rounded shape. Silver Lupine (*L. albifrons*) (fig. 53, pl. 5*c*), with its silky silver leaves, is represented locally by several forms. The spikelike racemes of lavender-purple flowers are seen on open wooded slopes in spring. The other two shrubby lupines are more commonly seen adjacent to the ocean on dunes or inland up

[45]

broad creek bottoms and inlets. The Yellow Bush Lupine (*L. arboreus*) (fig. 54), has been photographed for many a colored postcard. The leaves are not noticeably silky. Much variation in color occurs. Plants with lilac or blue-violet flowers are often seen that are but color forms.

Chamisso Bush Lupine (*L. chamissonis*) (fig. 55), which is found almost entirely on sand dunes from Marin County southward, is a more hairy shrub, with leaves and stems quite densely so. The petioles are short. The flowers are shades of purple.

Fig. 55 Chamisso Bush Lupine   Fig. 56 Deerweed

Deerweed (*Lotus scoparius*), fig 56.

One of the local species of lotus, though on the borderline, like milkwort, some penstemons, and Coyote Mint (*Monardella*), between perennial herbs and shrubs, is included as a sub-shrub in McMinn's *Illustrated Manual of California Shrubs*. Deerweed has numerous slim stems thickly bunched from ground level much like those of Rock-rose (*Helianthemum*). The tiny yellow pealike flowers are clustered in the leaf axils and can be found over a long blooming period. The small two-seeded pods are tipped by a curved beak. It is common in shrubby growth and woodland.

Broom (*Cytisus*)

The brooms grow easily and several kinds are planted in local gardens. They seed readily and, as the species are well suited to the central California climate, will spread to surrounding slopes. French Broom (*Cytisus monspessulanus*) (fig. 57), is particularly well acclimated; whole hillsides are colored in spring by its yellow flowers. The small pea-shaped flowers occur in small clusters among the abundant clover-like leaves. Scotch Broom (*C. scoparius*) has larger yellow flowers (about ¾ of an inch long) and strongly angled green stems that tend to be leafless. The pods are black. It, too, colors roadside slopes in spring. Spanish Broom (*Spartium junceum*) belongs to a related genus. It is less common in the wild than the two preceding. The large fragrant yellow flowers are clustered in loose racemes on the weak, leafless rush-like branches.

Gorse or Furze (*Ulex europeus*)

Like the brooms, gorse is an introduced European shrub and, unlike them, is a bad pest on coastal grazing land. Gorse is intricately branched and makes impenetrable thickets. It grows 3 to 6 feet high. All parts of this dingy, dark green shrub are spiny, except the small yellow flowers. The leaves are needle-pointed and all branches end in spines.

California False Indigo (*Amorpha californica napensis*)

The local variety of this inconspicuous shrub is sparingly distributed in the Coast Range around the Bay. Leaves are deciduous, about 5 to 10 inches long, and each leaf has about 20 small glandular leaflets along the rachis (central structure on which the leaflets are paired). The purple flowers are tiny and closely set along the slender spike. The dark pods are about ¼ of an inch long. It can be sought on dry brushy slopes in the northern coastal counties.

Fig. 57 French Broom

Fig. 58 California Hazelnut

Fig. 59 Interior Live Oak

Fig. 60 Golden Chinquapin

BIRCH FAMILY (Betulaceae)

California Hazelnut (*Corylus cornuta californica*), fig. 58.

This is a loose spreading shrub with simple saw-toothed deciduous leaves. The male and female flowers are separate: the pollen-bearing male flowers hang in long aments (slender compact clusters of flowers without petals like those of oaks, willows, or silktassel); the female flowers are solitary on joints of the stem and may be identified by their bright red stigmas. The shrub is common on moist north-facing slopes and in canyons. Occasional plants in open spaces may have short compact branches as a result of continued browsing by deer.

OAK OR BEECH FAMILY (Fagaceae)

Oaks are generally classed as trees, but at least two of the local species can truly be called shrubs. Shrubby forms of oak trees are always found, but these aberrant forms can usually be explained by stump sprouting or overcrowding in forest or chaparral. Low forms of each of the evergreen live oaks are named varieties: *Quercus agrifolia frutescens* (Coast Live Oak) and *Q. wislizenii frutescens* (Interior Live Oak) (fig. 59).

Both of the "shrub" oaks are of fairly common occurrence in the chaparral which is so prominent on much of the Inner Coast Range and the inner slopes of the Outer Coast Range. Leather Oak (*Q. durata*), an evergreen bush about 4 to 6 feet high, has oval leaves, convex on top, with the somewhat spiny margin rolled under; it is restricted in its habitat to serpentine. California Scrub Oak (*Q. dumosa*) has plane or rather wavy leaves, with the leaf margin visible; it is not limited to serpentine.

Golden Chinquapin (*Castanopsis chrysophylla minor*), fig. 60.

Although this variety of the Giant Chinquapin is always listed in books on shrubs, it is more often tree-like in form and grows to a height of 15 to 25 feet. It is distinguished by golden-backed evergreen leaves and chestnut-like burs which contain the hard-shelled seeds. The scientific name *Castanopsis* means castanea-like, in other words, a genus that resembles the chestnut. The burlike fruit looks like a real chestnut bur. They occur in groves in the higher elevations in the Outer Coast Range in mixed evergreen forests and closed-cone pine forests.

WAX-MYRTLE FAMILY (Myricaceae)

Pacific or **California Wax-myrtle** (*Myrica californica*), fig. 61.

This is a leafy evergreen shrub which in spite of its

brushy growth is often called a small tree. The clumps are often quite tall, growing to a height of more than 6 feet. The dark green leaves are somewhat aromatic, but not strongly so like the California Bay (*Umbellularia*) leaves which they strongly resemble. The male and female flowers are separate but grow on the same plant (monoecious). The small clusters of "berries" are purplish brown and have only a very light coating of wax. Wax-myrtle is found within the fog belt along the coast.

Fig. 61 Pacific Wax-myrtle   Fig. 62 Coulter Willow

WILLOW FAMILY (Salicaceae)
Willow (*Salix*)

Willows to survive must grow in well-watered areas —streambanks, wet meadows, springs, lakes, or arroyos. There is great similarity in the appearance of our species. Once the essential characters of the genus are recognized the amateur botanist will know the genus *Salix* at sight quite as readily as he knows the genus *Rosa*. The different species of willows, however, whether trees or shrubs, are not easy to tell apart. The male and the female flowers are borne on separate plants (dioecious) and come before or soon after the leaves. Both kinds of flowers are in aments or catkins, each flower with only a scale instead of a calyx or corolla under the essential parts of the flower. The

[50]

catkins are deciduous. The leaves are alternate and deciduous, and often turn brownish yellow before they fall. The typical leaf shape approaches a narrow ellipse. The shape varies among the species to linear or lanceolate (broadest at the basal end and tapering to a point) or oblanceolate (broadest toward the apex instead of at the base). The minute seeds, each with a fluff of "cotton," are packed in the small capsules of the female catkins and spread readily in the wind.

The regional willows that are commonly classed as trees are the Red Willow (*Salix laevigata*), the Yellow Willow (*S. lasiandra*), and the Valley Willow (*S. gooddingii*); the last is represented by a variety on the valley side of the Bay counties. Even these trees, confusingly, are occasionally found in a shrublike state. All the willows of the Bay Region, with the exception of Brewer Willow, are described as shrubs or small trees in the manuals and floras. The species given below are taken from the *Illustrated Manual of California Shrubs*.

The Brewer Willow (*S. breweri*) is a low bushy shrub with dull green leaves that grows not at all abundantly in poorly watered ravines in the Inner Coast Range from Santa Clara County to Napa County.

The Coulter or Velvet Willow (*S. coulteri*) (fig. 62) is a streambank willow of coastal counties of our area. Its rather coarse leaves are characterized by a dense white satiny covering of hair on the undersurface. The upper surface is green. The Sitka Willow (*S. sitchensis*), which grows as far south as Sonoma County, has more slender and nearly hairless branchlets and leaves that are typically rounded at the apex. Look for both species along streams on the ocean side of the Coast Ranges.

The Sandbar Willow (*S. hindsiana*) (fig. 63) commonly grows in dense thickets along sandbars and

Fig. 63 Sandbar Willow   Fig. 64 California Dutchman's
Pipe

ditches in the Inner Coast Range and warmer areas
of the Outer. It has slender stems, and the 1½ to
3 inch pale gray leaves are as narrow as grass blades.
It can become a tree with furrowed bark.

The Arroyo Willow (*S. lasiolepis*) is by far the
most common willow throughout the Bay Region and
with Scouler Willow the only ones (among ours)
on which the catkins appear before the leaves. The
leaves are highly variable in shape, but are never narrow like those of the Sandbar Willow. The underside
of the leaf is consistently paler than the upper side.

The Dusky Willow (*S. melanopsis*) grows from
the Rocky Mountains west to the northern Coast
Range and the Sierra Nevada. It merely touches the
Bay Region in Sonoma, Contra Costa, and Santa Clara
counties. The narrow leaves (to 3 inches long) are
dark green and lustrous above and paler but not
hairy beneath. It is sometimes called Long-leaf
Willow.

The Scouler Willow (*S. scouleriana*) can be classed
as a shrub, but sometimes within the limits of the Bay
counties is a white-barked tree 30 feet high. There
is much variation in the leaves throughout its extensive distribution from the Rocky Mountain chain to
the Pacific Ocean. They are always broadest above
the middle, often rounded at the apex, and ⅓ or
¼ as wide as they are long. The undersurface may
have silvery hairs or be covered with a whitish bloom.

[52]

Two northern willows, the Dune Willow (*S. piperi*) and the Coast Willow (*S. hookeriana*), occur as far south as Mendocino County on dunes and about lagoons and may yet be found farther south along the coast. Both have rather large leaves up to 4 inches long. The Dune Willow has shiny dark brown twigs; the Coast Willow, densely hairy ones.

California Fuchsia (*Zauschneria*) of the Evening Primrose family (*Onagraceae*) is sometimes listed in shrub books. It is a perennial herb with thin leafy stems, often a little woody at the base. In summer the bright red inch-long trumpets are very showy among the gray leaves.

BIRTHWORT FAMILY (Aristolochiaceae)

California Dutchman's Pipe or **Pipe Vine** (*Aristolochia californica*), fig. 64, pl. 5*d*.

This is the only California representative of that vine, so common elsewhere in the world, that bears such unusual flowers. It is a semiwoody vine climbing to a height of 6 to 12 feet. The leaves, 1½ to 5 inches long, are heart-shaped, alternate on the stem, and deciduous. The pipe-shaped flowers, formed by three fused sepals, hang pendant from the leaf axils. They are green tinged with purple. The vine is occasional along streambanks, but its occurrence south of San Francisco County has not been authenticated by recent collections.

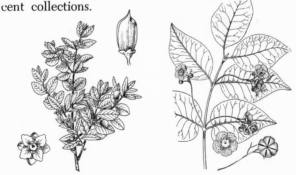

Fix 65 Oregon Boxwood   Fig. 66 California Burning Bush

STAFF-TREE FAMILY (Celastraceae)

All native plants of this family that occur in California are woody. Two of them occur in the Bay Region. One is extremely rare and finds its southern limit in Marin County. Oregon Boxwood or Mountain Lover (*Paxistima myrsinites*) (fig. 65) is a low branching shrub, seldom over 3 feet high, with slender stems thickly set with small evergreen leaves. The flowers with their greenish or purplish petals are inconspicuous, as are the small dry seed capsules. If observed at all, it will be found in coniferous (pines, Douglas Fir, fir, redwood) forests. It has been collected on Mount Tamalpais in Marin County.

California Burning Bush (*Euonymus occidentalis*), fig. 66.

The second genus, although not growing in close stands, is much more frequent than the preceding. The stems are long and flexible. The well-spaced deciduous leaves look much like prune-tree leaves; the long-stalked flowers are maroon; the horizontally depressed, lobed capsule splits when ripe down the center of each lobe, exposing the seeds embedded in reddish material which is known as an aril. It is found on shaded north-facing slopes and streambanks in the redwood and closed-cone pine forests.

GRAPE FAMILY (Vitaceae)

California Wild Grape (*Vitis californicus*), fig. 67.

Particularly in the counties north of San Francisco Bay the native wild grape vines are often seen blanketing even the taller trees. In autumn the leaves turn to a pinkish tone before they fall. The tiny greenish petals of the fragrant clustered flowers drop early. The bloom-covered grapes are too seedy for eating but make excellent jelly. The cultivated grape (*V. vinifera*), which sometimes escapes from vineyards in the wine country, can be distinguished from the native species by its young shoots, which are smooth

Fig. 67 California Wild Grape   Fig. 68 California Coffeeberry

instead of cobwebby. Should these plants bear fruit, the skin of the berry will adhere to the flesh instead of slipping off easily as it does in the wild grape.

BUCKTHORN FAMILY (Rhamnaceae)

Two of the genera of the buckthorn family and their several species form a very important part of the shrub flora of the Bay Region. Both have evergreen leaves which are noticeably feather-veined.

Coffeeberry or **Buckthorn** (*Rhamnus*)

The rather large, open-branched shrubs of California Coffeeberry (*R. californica*) (fig. 68) and two of its subspecies (*R. californica crassifolia* and *R. c. tomentella*) are easily distinguished from the Red-berried Buckthorn or Redberry (*R. crocea* and *R. crocea ilicifolia*) by leaves as well as berries. Coffeeberry has black berries, and the upper surface of the large elliptic, flexible evergreen leaves is dull green; that of the other species has a shining upper surface and a firm leathery texture. (Smaller-leaved variants can be found, usually in rocky open places.) The two subspecies of the California Coffeeberry which grow typically on inland slopes have rather bluish leaves which are short-hairy on the undersurface. The bushes of *R. crocea* (fig. 69) are much branched, with the branches rigid and often ending in a stout spine.

It has been mistakenly suggested that Cascara Sagrada (*R. purshiana*) enters the Bay Region at the northern coastal border in Sonoma County. However, this northern species, characterized by large deciduous leaves, grows only as far south as Mendocino County, and has been confused with large-leaved variations of *R. californica* which are often seen in closed-cone pine forests.

Ceanothus (*Ceanothus*) °

These woody plants, known as "California Lilac" when one is speaking of its taller kinds only, have more species in California than any other native genus except perhaps the manzanitas (*Arctostaphylos*). Both of these genera reach their highest development in this state. Of the California Lilac, forty-three species grow within the state's boundaries according to *A California Flora* by Philip A. Munz. This number does not include all the varietal names and named hybrids of this attractive genus, which has of recent years become more and more useful to western horticulturalists. There are twenty-seven named forms, counting all the species, varieties, and named hybrids growing within the Bay Region, and some hybrids have never been named. Many natural hybrids exist, owing to cross pollination between different species.

The species of *Ceanothus* fall naturally into two groups: species of the section *Euceanothus* have alternate leaves on the branchlets; three-lobed capsules without hornlike processes (sometimes with small thickened ridges or crests); and umbellate clusters of flowers arranged in close or open panicles. The species of the section *Cerastes* have very thick, rigid opposite leaves on the branchlets; lobes of the capsules with hornlike or thickened, warty processes; and flower umbels (flower stalks all arising from a central point) scattered among the leaves.

°For a definitive study of this genus see M. van Rensselaer and H. E. McMinn, *Ceanothus* (Santa Barbara Botanic Garden, Santa Barbara, 1942).

Fig. 69 *Rhamnus crocea*

Fig. 70 Tobacco Bush

Fig. 71 Deer-brush

Fig. 72 Carmel Ceanothus

Fig. 73 Parry Ceanothus

Fig. 74 Wart-leaf Ceanothus

[57]

Section *Euceanothus* (*Euceanothus*)

The most common local species of the section of *Euceanothus* is Blue Blossom and its various forms, although none of the other species actually are rare except Tobacco Bush, which grows on higher slopes north of the Bay.

Stems flexible or, if at all firm, not having branches ending in a spiny tip.

Leaves 1 inch or more wide (about ¾ the length), aromatic, having "varnished" upper surface; flowers white....................Tobacco Bush or Varnish-leaf Ceanothus(*Ceanothus velutinus laevigatus*), fig. 70

Leaves narrower in relation to length; flowers shades of blue; (Deer-brush white flowered).

Leaves deciduous or partly so, plane, very thin; flowers white (blue or pink variants rare)................ Deer-brush (*C. integerrimus*), fig. 71

Leaves evergreen, quite firm, often glandular, having margins rolled under.

Branches and branchlets ridged longitudinally or prominently angled......Blue Blossom (*C. thyrsiflorus* and vars.), pl. 6*a*, Carmel Ceanothus (*C. griseus*), fig. 72, Parry Ceanothus (*C. parryi*), fig. 73

Branches and branchlets round, branchlets with very short hairs............Wavy-leaf Ceanothus (*C. foliosus* and vars.), Wart-leaf Ceanothus (*C. papillosus* and forms), fig. 74 Crop-leaf Ceanothus (*C. dentatus*)

Stems rigid, ending in stout thornlike spines or at least stiffly spreading and not flexible in Jim-brush; stems chalky or pale green.

Flowers white..........Coastal Whitethorn (*C. incanus*), fig. 75, Chaparral Whitethorn (*C. leucodermis*), pl. 6*b*.

Flowers pale to deeper blue....Jim-brush (*C. sorediatus*), fig. 76

Section *Cerastes*

The most easily recognized and the most common, locally as well as elsewhere in the state, is Buckbrush (*Ceanothus cuneatus*) (pl. 6*c*). The leaves have entire margins and the flowers are white. The other kinds in

Fig. 75 Coastal Whitethorn

Fig. 76 Jim-brush

Fig. 77 Coast Ceanothus

Fig. 78 Jepson's Ceanothus

Fig. 79 Point Reyes Ceanothus

Fig. 80 Coyote Ceanothus

SPECIES OF CEANOTHUS

Species	Habitat	Distribution
Ceanothus cuneatus	chaparral, foothill woodland, dry interior slopes	very common in California, Inner Coast Range, inner slopes of Outer Coast Range
C. dentatus	closed-cone pine forest, chaparral, mixed evergreen forest	limited, Santa Cruz. Co. south to San Luis Obispo Co.
C. divergens	chaparral, foothill woodland	limited to Napa Co., not common
C. divergens confusus	chaparral	limited, north Sonoma Co., Napa Co. to Lake Co., not common
C. ferrisiae	chaparral, foothill woodland	limited, Mt. Hamilton Range, Santa Clara Co., Santa Cruz Mts., San Mateo Co.
C. foliosus	mixed evergreen forest, yellow-pine forest, chaparral	Coast Ranges south from Humboldt Co. to Santa Cruz Co.
C. foliosus vineatus	chaparral	local, Sonoma Co.
C. foliosus medius	coastal scrub	Mt. Hamilton Range, Santa Clara Co.
C. gloriosus	coastal scrub	limited, Marin Co. to Mendocino Co.
C. gloriosus exaltatus	closed-cone pine forest	limited, Marin Co. to Mendocino Co.
C. gloriosus porrectus	closed-cone pine forest, coastal scrub	limited to Marin Co.
C. griseus	redwood forest, mixed evergreen forest	Sonoma Co. to Mendocino Co., also south Coast Ranges
C. incanus	mixed evergreen forest; yellow-pine forest	Outer Coast Range, Santa Cruz Co. north to Humboldt Co.
C. integerrimus		Inner Coast Range, Santa Cruz Co., common elsewhere in California

C. *jepsonii*	serpentine chaparral	limited, Marin Co. to Mendocino Co.
C. *jepsonii albiflorus*		Napa Co.
C. *leucodermis*	chaparral, foothill woodland	Inner Coast Range, Santa Clara Co. to Alameda Co., common elsewhere in California
C. *masonii*	chaparral	very local, Marin Co.
C. *papillosus*	mixed evergreen forest, redwood forest, chaparral	Outer Coast Range, San Mateo Co. to San Luis Obispo Co.
C. *regius*	hybrid	very local, San Mateo Co.
C. *parryi*	mixed evergreen forest, redwood forest	Napa Co. and Sonoma Co. to Humboldt Co.
C. *prostratus occidentalis*	yellow-pine forest	Sonoma Co. and Napa Co, north to Mendocino Co. and Lake Co.
C. *purpureus*	chaparral	Napa Co.
C. *ramulosus*	chaparral	Outer Coast Range, Santa Barbara Co. north to Mendocino Co.
C. *sonomensis*	chaparral	very local, Sonoma Co.
C. *sorediatus*	chaparral, foothill woodland	Coast Ranges in Bay Region, common elsewhere in California
C. *thyrsiflorus*	chaparral, redwood forest, mixed evergreen forest	common, Outer Coast Range, Santa Barbara Co. to Oregon border, very common in Bay Region
C. *thyrsiflorus repens*	coastal scrub	occasional, Marin Co. south
C. *velutinus laevigatus*	mixed evergreen forest, redwood forest	not common locally, Outer Coast Range, Marin Co. north

this section have pale or dark blue or lavender flowers, with the exception of Coyote Ceanothus (*C. ferrisiae*) and white variants of the other species. An
entire leaf margin is the exception among the species
with colored flowers, if one omits Coast Ceanothus
(*C. ramulosus*) (fig. 77). Even that is sometimes
found to have a slightly serrate margin. The appearance of the toothed-margin leaves is variable. The
leaves may suggest miniature holly leaves as do Jepson's Ceanothus (*C. jepsonii*) (fig. 78), and Napa
Ceanothus (*C. purpureus*), or more and shorter teeth
as do the leaves of Point Reyes Ceanothus (*C. gloriosus*) (fig. 79).

Height helps to a small degree in separating the
species. Floras and manuals should be checked for
detailed information.

Species that are 3 to 9 feet high: Buckbrush (*C.
cuneatus*), Coyote Ceanothus (*C. ferrisiae*) (fig. 80),
Coast Ceanothus (*C. ramulosus*), Bolinas Ceanothus
(*C. masonii*), Sonoma Ceanothus (*C. sonomensis*),
Point Reyes Ceanothus (*C. gloriosus exaltatus*), Napa
Ceanothus (*C. purpureus*).

Species that are low-growing (6 to 24 inches),
either creeping or having low arching branches: Cali-
stoga Ceanothus (*C. divergens* and var. *C. divergens
confusus*), Jepson's Ceanothus (*C. jepsonii*), Point
Reyes Ceanothus (*C. gloriosus* and *C. gloriosus por-
rectus*, which is prostrate), Western Squaw-mat (*C.
prostratus occidentalis*).

MEZEREUM FAMILY (Thymelaeaceae)

Leatherwood (*Dirca occidentalis*), fig. 81 (see cover)
These Shrubs are 2½ to 3½ feet high, with smooth
brown stems that are completely pliant. The bright
yellow calyces (no corollas) set closely in the axils of
the simple leaves, and from the flowers develop yellowish green fruits (drupes), each with a single
seed. The deciduous leaves have the shape of a nar-

Fig. 81 Leatherwood   Fig. 82 Western Hop Tree

row ellipse and look like thin willow leaves. Leatherwood grows in mixed chaparral and woodland and is not very common. It is native to Coastal Bay Region counties only.

The mistletoes (*Phoradendron*) are sometimes included among the shrubs, but are omitted in this book.

RUE FAMILY (Rutaceae)

The rue family is known to the public by the genus *Citrus* (orange, lemon, lime, etc.). Only four genera (one garden escape) grow in California without cultivation. Only one is found in the Bay Region.

Western Hop Tree (*Ptelea crenulata*), fig. 82, pl. 6d.
This shrub or small tree grows in canyons and flats of the Inner Coast Range from Mount Diablo southward and is not common. The deciduous leaves are gland-dotted and ill-smelling, and each leaf is divided into three leaflets like those of the clovers (trifoliate). The greenish white clustered flowers are inconspicuous. The dry fruits are encircled by a membranous wing.

SUMAC FAMILY (Anacardiaceae)

Poison Oak (*Rhus diversiloba*), fig. 83, pl. 7a.
Poison Oak is a versatile plant. It forms clumps 2 feet or more in height, and thickets even higher, or

it may be a woody vine climbing like ivy up the trunks of trees. It gives the local foothills their best fall color before the brilliant red trifoliate leaves drop, but with dry leaves or fresh new leaves it is a plant to avoid as it gives most people a dermatitis which is often very severe. The small green flowers which appear with the leaves hang in loose clusters as do the small dry fruit. It grows very abundantly in all sorts of habitats. It is not to be confused with Poison Ivy or Poison Sumac, which are native to the eastern United States. A related species growing in arroyo bottoms and flats is Squaw-bush (*R. trilobata*). The velvety leaves look much like those of Poison Oak, but this one is safe to touch. The shrub has flexible stems 2 to 3 feet high, and the ripening fruit (slightly fleshy, with a sticky secretion) is orange-red.

English Ivy (*Hedera helix*), a well-known woody vine of the ginseng family, occasionally grows spontaneously in the wild. It has undoubtedly been spread by birds, for they seem to like the black berries.

Fig. 83 Poison Oak   Fig. 84 Brown Dogwood

Dogwood Family (Cornaceae)

Brown Dogwood (*Cornus glabrata*), fig. 84.

This shrub is frequently found in moist situations

on north-facing wooded slopes or along streambanks
from north to south in the Bay Region. It grows 4 to
15 feet high, and is much branched. The deciduous
pointed leaves are opposite on the smooth reddish
brown twigs. The small white flowers grow in small
clusters on the flower stalk. The white drupes (fleshy
fruits with one central stone) serve as bird food and
disappear quickly.

Western Dogwood (*Cornus occidentalis*), fig. 85, pl.
7*b*.

This is a more erect, less branching shrub often found
in clumps by streambeds where it occurs frequently
throughout the area. In its leafless stage the rich red
stems make a finer display than they do in their leafy
stage. The leaves are similar to those of Brown Dogwood, but are longer (up to 3½ inch) and have
more prominent veins. Flowers and fruits are much
the same.

Fig. 85 Western Dogwood   Fig. 86 Coast Silktassel

SILKTASSEL FAMILY (Garryaceae)

Silktassel Bush (*Garrya*)

The silktassels give the earliest blooms on the chaparral slopes. The pendant aments of the staminate flowers of the Coast Silktassel (*G. elliptica*) (fig. 86)
can be found as early as late January, about
the time when hazelnuts and alders are putting out
their similar hanging aments. The sexes are never

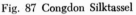

Fig. 87 Congdon Silktassel   Fig. 88 Buttonbush

found on the same bush—always on separate ones. The four species that occur within our range all have leathery leaves, are evergreen, and grow in chaparral, coastal scrub, or areas where mixed foothill woodland approaches the chaparral area. The leaves of two of the species have wavy, undulate, but entire margins: Coast Silktassel (*G. elliptica*) and Congdon Silktassel (*G. congdonii*) (fig. 87). On the other two species the whole leaf is flat and plane and the margin is also entire: Fremont Silktassel (*G. fremontii*) and Ashy Silktassel (*G. flavescens pallida*). Fremont Silktassel has yellowish green leaves and black fruits almost devoid of hair. All the others have grayish or ashy leaves and more or less densely silky fruits. Coast Silktassel is most frequently seen. Even this species, though common in the Outer Coast Range, is not found growing in stands in any one place but as solitary individual plants in chaparral. The other three are more characteristic of the Inner Coast Range. Ashy Silktassel is reported from Alameda County; Congdon Silktassel grows in Napa County southward through the Mount Hamilton Range; Fremont Silktassel grows in Marin County (Mount Tamalpais) and in Santa Clara County on Loma Prieta as well as the Mount Hamilton Range.

[66]

MADDER FAMILY (Rubiaceae)

Buttonbush or **Button Willow** (*Cephalanthus occidentalis*), fig. 88.

This large shrub grows by sloughs and living streams. As it grows best in warm interior valleys, it is rarely seen in the Bay counties and then only along watercourses of the Inner Coast Range adjacent to the Sacramento—San Joaquin Valley. The simple leaves are large, opposite, and deciduous. The ball-shaped heads of cream-colored flowers appear in the summer months, and each flower develops into a hard, dry capsule.

HONEYSUCKLE FAMILY (Caprifoliaceae)

Corolla lobes spreading flatly like spokes of a wheel.
    Leaves compound with 3 to 7 leaflets.................
                           Elderberry (*Sambucus*)
    Leaves simple with margin toothed, sometimes shallowly
    lobed..........................Viburnum (*Viburnum*)
Corolla lobes shorter than corolla tube or, if as long or longer, corollas two-lipped and lobes recurved inward toward tube.
    Leaves deciduous; erect shrubs; flowers tubular or trumpet-shaped, with short flaring lobes.
        Berries white, spongy, not shining; flowers pinkish or
        pinkish white............Snowberry (*Symphoricarpos*)
        Berries black, shining; flowers yellow or reddish
        tinged..............Twinberry (*Lonicera involucrata*)
    Leaves evergreen; slender woody vines or plants with short, erect trunks and climbing or reclining stems and branches; flowers two-lipped.
        Corollas pink or purplish; slender-stemmed vines.......
        Hairy or California Honeysuckle (*L. hispidula vacillans*)
        Corollas pale yellow or reddish; weak stems from
        woody trunk...............Southern Honeysuckle (*L.
                  subspicata johnstoni*), Chaparral
                  Honeysuckle (*L. interrupta*)

Snowberry (*Symphoricarpos*)

The two species of snowberry can be distinguished by their growth form. Common Snowberry (*S. albus laevigatus*, sometimes under the name *S. rivularis*) (fig. 89), grows from 2 to 6 feet high and is erect

Fig. 89 Common Snowberry

Fig. 90 Viburnum

Fig. 91 Coast Elderberry

Fig. 92 Blue Elderberry

Fig. 93 Twinberry

Fig. 94 California Honeysuckle

and slender-branched. Creeping Snowberry (*S. mollis*) is also slender-branched, but is seldom more than a foot high, and the branches are diffuse, sometimes creeping. Both have pinkish flowers and both grow on wooded slopes and are quite common throughout the Bay area.

Viburnum (*Viburnum ellipticum*) (fig. 90)   occurs rarely. It has been collected in Contra Costa and Sonoma counties. The clustered flowers are white; the drupes (stone fruit like prunes or peaches) are black.

Elderberry (*Sambucus*)

There are blue elderberries and red elderberries. Both have cream-colored flowers. The Coast or Red Elderberry has a tightly branched, dome-shaped inflorescence, and grows on slopes and streambeds draining directly into the sea, from central California northward. It is recognized by some as a distinct species, *S. callicarpa*; by others as a western variety, *S. pubens arborescens* (pl. 7c, fig. 91).

The branches of the inflorescence of the Blue or Desert Elderberry (*S. mexicana*) (fig. 92, pl. 7d) are spreading and present a flat-topped rather than a dome-shaped appearance. The dark berries are covered with a whitish bloom. *Sambucus mexicana* is a variable species, as can be seen in the shape and surface of its sometimes velvety leaflets. It may take on a treelike form 25 to 30 feet tall. Although the Blue Elderberry is found in the Bay Region near the coast, it is more frequently found in the Inner Coast Range, and grows at lower elevations southward to Mexico. It is a common sight along streamcourses and in open woodland.

Honeysuckle (*Lonicera*)

If one counts the Garden Honeysuckle, which occasionally persists without cultivation, there are five species of *Lonicera* in the Bay Region (see family key). Twinberry (fig. 93) is an erect, yellow-flowered

shrub of the fog belt, and California or Hairy Honeysuckle, (fig. 94), too, thrives best in a cool climate.
The other two species, which are half woody and half
climbing on other shrubs, prefer the hot Inner Coast
Range.

Fig. 95 Eastwoodia   Fig. 96 Bush Yarrow

SUNFLOWER FAMILY (Compositae)

Taking a worldwide view, this is one of the largest
plant families. In California alone there are 180 genera and hundreds of species and varieties. Low-growing annuals and perennials belonging to the sunflower
family abound in the Bay Region, but the number
of species classed as shrubs are few. What appears to
be a single flower in this plant family is really a modi-
fied head of many flowers (see page 6). Only three
of the local shrubs have ray flowers ¾ to 1 inch
long;* all the others lack ray flowers surrounding the
central mass of disk flowers, or have short rays ¼
of an inch long or less.

Eastwoodia or **Yellow Mock-Aster** (*Eastwoodia elegans*), fig. 95.

This rounded leafy bush, with rayless yellow flower

*Shrubby Butterwort or Bush Groundsel (*Senecio douglasii*),
Marsh Grindelia (*Grindelia humilis*), Goldenbush (*Haplopappus linearifolius*).

heads, grows only on the hot, dry hills on the San Joaquin Valley side of the Inner Coast Range and barely touches Alameda and eastern Santa Clara counties, an area where several more southerly shrubs of the Great Valley might yet be found.

Lizard Tail or **Seaside Woolly-Aster** (*Eriophyllum staechadifolium*), pl. 8*a*.

On bluffs and dunes along the shoreline of the coastal counties the leafy mounds of Lizard Tail are frequently found. They may grow to a height of 3 feet. The gray leaves (becoming greenish in age) are much divided, but there is a form with undivided leaves. Because of the soft, brittle though woody lower stems, this plant could just as well be classed as a woody-based perennial plant. The same can be said of two other species of *Eriophyllum* often listed among California shrubs: *E. jepsonii* (Bush Yarrow) (fig. 96), of the Mount Diablo area, and *E. confertiflorum* (Golden Yarrow), a foot-high compact "shrub" that is common in mixed chaparral.

Marsh Grindelia or **Gum Plant** (*Grindelia humilis*), fig. 97.

This shrubby plant grows only in the salt marshes. The resinous stickiness of the foliage has an almost medicinal odor. The conspicuous flower heads bloom from late summer into autumn. Several herbaceous

Fig. 97 Marsh Grindelia   Fig. 98 Mock Heather

species occur in the Bay Region in all sorts of habitats. Their flowers are much alike and give off the same resinous odor.

Goldenbush (*Haplopappus*)

Four shrubby species of this large and diverse genus grow in the Bay Region.

Flower heads with yellow rays (very short in Mock Heather).
  Rays 2 to 6, about ¼ of an inch long....................
    Mock Heather (*Haplopappus ericoides*)
  Rays 12 to 18, ½ to 1 inch long...Narrowleaf Goldenbush
    (*H. linearifolius*)
Flower heads without rays.
  Shrubs 3 to 12 feet high, fastigiately branched (branches in close, erect clusters) above, lower stems unbranched, leafless; bracts of flower heads sharply pointed, not noticeably green-tipped........Golden Fleece
    (*H. arborescens*)
  Shrubs 1½ to 3 feet high, bushy branching from base and above; bracts around flower heads rather broad, green-tipped........Coast Goldenbush (varieties of
    H. venetus)

Mock Heather (*H. ericoides*), fig. 98, pl. 8*b*.

The neatly shaped shrubs of Mock Heather have stems thickly set with needle-like leaves about ½ of an inch long, with still shorter leaves clustered in the leaf axils, thus strongly suggesting the heather of our gardens in appearance. However, the flowers are yellow and of a very different shape. It is common on the dunes near the coast. A subspecies (*H. ericoides blakei*), which differs only in some technical points, grows in sandy places behind the immediate coast.

Narrowleaf Goldenbush (*H. linearifolius*), fig. 99, pl. 8*c*.

This much-branched, rounded shrub can reach a height of 5 feet. The narrow leaves are dotted with glands and the young branchlets are resinous. The copious green foliage makes an excellent background for the large yellow flower heads which blossom in spring. It grows in the Inner Coast Range in our area.

Fig. 99 Goldenbush   Fig. 100 Golden Fleece

Golden Fleece (*H. arborescens*), fig. 100.

In summer, flowering Golden Fleece makes a colorful show on open, dry, wooded slopes or mixed chaparral, usually well away from the fog belt. The linear to threadlike leaves, 1 to 2½ inches long, have a fragrant aroma.

Coast Goldenbush (*H. venetus*, vars. *vernonioides* and *arguta*)

Both varieties of this goldenbush usually grow in somewhat alkaline or saline soil. The variety *arguta* is found in the salt-marsh area of Solano and Contra Costa counties. The variety *vernonioides* grows along the coast as far south as San Diego County. The leaves of both are rather thick, with either an entire or a toothed margin.

Rabbitbrush (*Chrysothamnus*)

Only one of the subspecies of the common rabbitbrush (*C. nauseosus mohavensis*) is found in the Bay Region. Others commonly occur in the desert and arid slopes in the West, and color the canyons and slopes with yellow in autumn or late summer. Ours occurs much more sparingly in the coastal mountains. It is readily spotted in the few places where it grows in the Bay Region (higher slopes on both sides of the Santa Clara Valley) by its gray foliage and late-blooming flower heads.

Coyote Bush, Chaparral Broom, or **Mule Fat** (*Baccharis*) The various species of *Baccharis* from here to South America are not easy to tell apart, but all have one characteristic that shows their kinship, whether they are shrubs or just perennials that are slightly woody at the base. The species are dioecious, with the staminate and the pistillate flowers on different plants.

Fig. 101 Mule Fat

Fig. 102 Coast Sagebrush

Fig. 103 Scale Broom

Fig. 104 Bush Groundsel

[74]

The flower heads of both are without rays and the flowers are white instead of yellow.

Leaf margins coarsely toothed at apex of leaf, entire margined at narrow base; flower heads clustered in leaf axils.
  Prostrate evergreen shrubs with rooting branches; plants of immediate seacoast......Dwarf Chaparral Broom
(*Baccharis pilularis pilularis*)
  Erect shrubby evergreen shrubs; common plants of Coast Range hills and valleys..Chaparral Broom or Coyote
Bush (*B. pilularis consanguinea*), pl. 8d.
Leaves linear or nearly so; flower heads in small leafless clusters at tips of stems and branches; willow-like thickets along streamcourses............Mule Fat (*B. viminea*), fig. 101

Salt Marsh Baccharis (*B. douglasii*), a herbaceous leafy-stemmed plant 3 to 6 feet high, is found in damp inland areas and often in salt marshes.

Coast Sagebrush or **Old Man** (*Artemisia californica*), fig. 102.

The compound leaves of the Coast Sagebrush are once or twice divided into threadlike segments. The rounded shrubs, 2 to 5 feet high, are found on open hillsides or mixed chaparral. The gray foliage has the same tangy aroma as the sagebrush of the Great Basin area.

Scale Broom (*Lepidospartum squamatum*), fig. 103.

This shrub is 3 to 6 feet high, with erect, broomlike branches and branchlets. Young shoots are leafy, with scalelike leaves clothing the stems. As with many other local shrubs of the sunflower family, the foliage and stems are gray. In the Bay Region it is found only in broad dry washes and gravels in the Inner Coast Range.

Bush Groundsel or **Bushy Butterweed** (*Senecio douglasii*), fig. 104.

This is an open, loosely branched shrub of the gravelly soil of flats and washes in the Inner Coast Range, but it is widely distributed in similar places throughout the state. The leaves are gray and have a few threadlike divisions. The flower heads are showy, with rays ½-inch long. The flowers appear in summer.

California Brickellia (*Brickellia californica*), fig. 105.

The shrubs are usually rather straggly and rarely reach a height of 3 feet. The stems and branches arise from the base and, though woody, are thin and brittle. The pleasantly fragrant leaves are broadly egg-shaped and the margins have rounded teeth. With the species of *Baccharis*, it has the distinction among the local shrubs of the sunflower family of having white instead of yellow flower heads. It grows on dry canyon walls and streambeds, and is more commonly found in the Inner Coast Range. California Brickellia is widely distributed in the West.

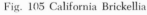

Fig. 105 California Brickellia   Fig. 106 Greenbriar

LILY FAMILY (Liliaceae)

Greenbriar (*Smilax californica*), fig. 106.

The only shrubby member of the lily family in the Bay Region is the woody vine known as Greenbriar. Another woody lily, Spanish Bayonet or Our Lord's Candle, merely approaches our southern border in Monterey and San Benito counties. Greenbriar is a native of southwestern Oregon and the northern coastal ranges of California, and has been found as far south as Napa County. The woody, often prickly stems can climb to 9 feet by means of tendrils. The broad, rather heart-shaped leaves are deciduous though tardily so, and are usually lacking at the base. Small greenish flowers are in the stalked clusters in the leaf axils, and staminate and pistillate flowers are on separate plants. The ripened berries are black and about ¼ of an inch in diameter.

CHECK LIST OF NATIVE SHRUBS
OF THE SAN FRANCISCO BAY REGION

CALYCANTHUS FAMILY (Calycanthaceae)
Calycanthus occidentalis, Spicebush, p. 13, pl. 1*a*.

BUTTERCUP FAMILY (Ranunculaceae)
Clematis lasiantha, Chaparral Clematis, p. 14, pl. 1*b*.
Clematis ligusticifolia, Western Virgin's Bower, p. 14, pl. 1*c*.

BARBERRY FAMILY (Berberidaceae)
Mahonia dictyota, Jepson's Mahonia, p. 15.
Mahonia nervosa, Long-leaf Mahonia, p. 14.
Mahonia pinnata, Shiny-leaf Mahonia, pp. 14–15.

CACAO OR STERCULIA FAMILY (Sterculiaceae)
Fremontodendron californicum, Flannel-bush, p. 15, pl. 1*d*.

MALLOW FAMILY (Malvaceae)
Lavatera arborea, Tree Mallow, p. 16.
Lavatera assurgentiflora, Malva Rosa, p. 17.
Malacothamnus arcuatus, p. 16.
Malacothamnus fremontii, p. 16.
Malacothamnus hallii, p. 16.
Polygala californica, p. 17, pl. 2*a*.

SPURGE FAMILY (Euphorbiaceae)
Ricinus communis, Castor Bean, p. 17.

ROCK-ROSE FAMILY (Cistaceae)
Helianthemum scoparium, Rock-Rose, p. 18.

TAMARISK FAMILY (Tamaricaceae)
Tamarix tetrandra, p. 18.

FRANKENIA FAMILY (Frankeniaceae)
Frankenia grandifolia, Alkali-heath, p. 18.

POPPY FAMILY (Papaveraceae)
Dendromecon rigidum, Tree Poppy, p. 19, pl. 2*b*.

BUCKWHEAT FAMILY (Polygonaceae)
Eriogonum fasciculatum, California Buckwheat, p. 19.

GOOSEFOOT OR SALTBUSH FAMILY
(Chenopodiaceae)
Allenrolfea occidentalis, Bush Pickleweed, p. 21.
Atriplex lentiformis, Brewer's Salt Bush, p. 21.
Suaeda californica, California Sea-blite, p. 21.
Suaeda fruticosa, Alkali-blite, p. 21.

HEATHER FAMILY (Ericaceae)
Arctostaphylos spp., Manzanita, pp. 22–27 and pl. 3*a.*
Gaultheria shallon, p. 22.
Ledum glandulosum, Labrador Tea, pp. 22–23, pl. 2*d.*
Rhododendron occidentale, Western Azalea, p. 21.
Vaccinium ovatum, p. 23.
Vaccinium parvifolium, Red Huckleberry, p. 22, pl. 2*c.*

OLIVE FAMILY (Oleaceae)
Forestiera neomexicana, Desert Olive, p. 27.

WATERLEAF OR PHACELIA FAMILY
(Hydrophyllaceae)
Eriodictyon californicum, California Yerba Santa, p. 28,
pl. 3*b.*

NIGHTSHADE FAMILY (Solanaceae)
Nicotiana glauca, Tree Tobacco, p. 28.
Solanum aviculare, Poporo, p. 30.
Solanum marginatum, White-margined Nightshade, p. 30.
Solanum umbelliferum, Blue Nightshade, p. 29, pl. 3*c.*

FIGWORT FAMILY (Scrophulariaceae)
Mimulus aurantiacus, Sticky Monkeyflower, p. 30, pl. 3*d.*
Penstemon breviflorus, Gaping Penstemon, pp. 30–31,
pl. 4*a.*
Penstemon corymbosus, Redwood Penstemon, p. 30.

MINT FAMILY (Labiatae)
Lepechinia calycina, Pitcher Sage, p. 32, pl. 4*b.*
Salvia mellifera, Black Sage, p. 32.
Salvia sonomensis, Sonoma Sage, p. 32.

SAXIFRAGE FAMILY (Saxifragaceae)
Ribes spp., Gooseberries, Currants, pp. 33–36, pl. 4*c.*

ROSE FAMILY (Rosaceae)
Adenostoma fasciculatum, Chamise, p. 37.

Amelanchier pallida, Serviceberry, p. 42.
Cercocarpus betuloides, Mountain Mahogany, p. 37.
Crataegus douglasii, Hawthorn, p. 43.
Heteromeles arbutifolia, California Christmas Berry, p. 44.
Holodiscus discolor, Creambush, pp. 37–38.
Osomaronia cerasiformis, Osoberry, p. 42.
Physocarpus capitatus, Western Ninebark, pp. 37–38.
Prunus emarginata, Bitter Cherry, p. 42.
Prunus ilicifolia, Hollyleaf Cherry, p. 42.
Prunus subcordata, Sierra Plum, p. 42.
Prunus virginiana demissa, Western Chokecherry, p. 42.
Rosa californica, California Rose, p. 39, pl. 4*d*.
Rosa eglantina, Sweetbriar, p. 39.
Rosa gymnocarpa, Redwood Rose, p. 39.
Rosa pinetorum, Pine Rose, pp. 39–40.
Rosa spithamea sonomensis, Sonoma Ground Rose, p. 39.
Rubus spp., Blackberry, etc., pp. 40–41 and pl. 5*a*.

PEA FAMILY (Leguminosae)
Amorpha californica napensis, California False Indigo,
    p. 47.
Cercis occidentalis, Western Redbud, pp. 44–45.
Cytisus monspessulanus, French Broom, p. 47.
Cytisus scoparius, Scotch Broom, p. 47.
Lotus scoparius, Deerweed, p. 46.
Lupinus albifrons, Silver Lupine, p. 45, pl. 5*c*.
Lupinus arboreus, Yellow Bush Lupine, p. 46.
Lupinus chamissonis, Chamisso Bush Lupine, p. 46.
Pickeringia montana, Chaparral Pea, p. 45, pl. 5*b*.
Spartium junceum, Spanish Broom, p. 47.
Ulex europeus, Gorse, Furze, p. 47.

BIRCH FAMILY (Betulaceae)
Corylus cornuta californica, California Hazelnut, p. 48.

OAK OR BEECH FAMILY (Fagaceae)
Castanopsis chrysophylla minor, Golden Chinquapin, p. 49.
Quercus agrifolia frutescens, Coast Live Oak, p. 49.
Quercus dumosa, California Scrub Oak, p. 49.
Quercus durata, Leather Oak, p. 49.
Quercus wislizenii frutescens, Interior Live Oak, pl. 49.

WAX-MYRTLE FAMILY (Myricaceae)
Myrica californica, California Wax-Myrtle, pp. 49–50.

WILLOW FAMILY (Salicaceae)
Salix brewerii, Brewer Willow, p. 51.
Salix coulteri, Coulter Willow, p. 51.
Salix hindsiana, Sandbar Willow, pp. 51–52.
Salix hookeriana, Coast Willow, p. 53.
Salix lasiolepis, Arroyo Willow, p. 52.
Salix melanopsis, Dusky Willow, p. 52.
Salix piperi, Dune Willow, p. 53.
Salix scouleriana, Scouler Willow, p. 52.
Salix sitchensis, Sitka Willow, p. 52.

BIRTHWORT FAMILY (Aristolochiaceae)
Aristolochia californica, California Dutchman's Pipe, p. 53, pl. 5d.

STAFF-TREE FAMILY (Celastraceae)
Euonymus occidentalis, California Burning Bush, p. 54.
Paxistima myrsinites, Oregon Boxwood, p. 54.

GRAPE FAMILY (Vitaceae)
Vitis californicus, California Wild Grape, p. 54.

BUCKTHORN FAMILY (Rhamnaceae)
Ceanothus spp., "California Lilac," pp. 56–62, pls. 6a, b, and c.
Rhamnus californica, California Coffeeberry, p. 55.
Rhamnus crocea, Red-berried Buckthorn, p. 55.

MEZEREUM FAMILY (Thymelaeaceae)
Dirca occidentalis, Leatherwood, pp. 62–63, cover.

RUE FAMILY (Rutaceae)
Ptelea crenulata, Western Hop Tree, p. 63, pl. 6d.

SUMAC FAMILY (Anacardiaceae)
Rhus diversiloba, Poison Oak, pp. 63–64, pl. 7a.
Rhus trilobata, Squaw-bush, p. 64.

DOGWOOD FAMILY (Cornaceae)
Cornus glabrata, Brown Dogwood, pp. 64–65.
Cornus occidentalis, Western Dogwood, p. 65, pl. 7b.

SILKTASSEL FAMILY (Garryaceae)
Garrya congdonii, Congdon Silktassel, p. 66.
Garrya elliptica, Coast Silktassel, pp. 65–66.
Garrya flavescens pallida, Ashy Silktassel, p. 66
Garya fremontii, Fremont Silktassel, p. 66.

MADDER FAMILY (Rubiaceae)
Cephalanthus occidentalis, Buttonbush, p. 67.

HONEYSUCKLE FAMILY (Caprifoliaceae)
Lonicera involucrata, Twinberry, pp. 69–70.
Sambucus mexicana, Blue Elderberry, p. 69, pl. 7*d.*
Sambucus pubens arborescens, Coast Elderberry, p. 69, pl. 7*c.*
Symphoricarpos albus laevigatus, Common Snowberry, p. 67.
Symphoricarpos mollis, Creeping Snowberry, p. 69.
Viburnum ellipticum, Viburnum, p. 69.

SUNFLOWER FAMILY (Compositae)
Artemisia californica, Coast Sagebrush, p. 75.
Baccharis douglasii, Salt Marsh Baccharis, p. 75.
Baccharis pilularis consanguinea, Chaparral Broom, p. 75, pl. 8*d.*
*Baccharis pilularis pilularis,*Dwarf Chaparral Broom, p. 75.
Baccharis viminea, Mule Fat, p. 75.
Brickellia californica, California Brickellia, p. 76.
Chrysothamnus nauseosus mohavensis, Rabbitbrush, pp. 73–74.
Eastwoodia elegans, Eastwoodia, pp. 70–71.
Eriophyllum confertiflorum, Golden Yarrow, p. 71.
Eriophyllum jepsonii, Bush Yarrow, p. 71.
Eriophyllum staechadifolium, Lizard Tail, p. 71, pl. 8*a.*
Grindelia humilis, Marsh Grindelia, pp. 71–72.
Haplopappus arborescens, Golden Fleece, p. 73.
Haplopappus ericoides, Mock Heather, p. 72, pl. 8*b.*
Haplopappus linearifolius, Narrowleaf Goldenbush, p. 72, pl. 8*c.*
Haplopappus venetus, Coast Goldenbush, p. 73.
Lepidospartum squamatum, Scale Broom, p. 75.
Senecio douglasii, Bush Groundsel, pp. 75–76.

LILY FAMILY (Liliaceae)
Smilax californica, Greenbriar, pp. 76–77.